北京名胜揽萃
Spectacular Scenic Sights of Beijing

新星出版社
New Star Publishers

First Edition 2003

ISBN 7-80148-547-5

Copyright 2003 by New Star publishers, Beijing, China
Published by New Star Publishers
24 Baiwanzhuang Road, Beijing, 100037, China
Distributed by China International Book Trading Corporation
35 Chegongzhuang Xilu, Bejing, 100044, China
P.O.Box 399, Beijing,China

Printed in the People's Repblic of China

目 录 CONTENTS

前 言··4
Foreword··5

天安门广场
Tian'anmen Square··························6

故 宫
The Palace Museum·······················14

天 坛
The Temple of Heaven····················38

颐和园
The Summer Palace························52

长 城
The Great Wall······························74

明十三陵
The Ming Tombs····························90

北海公园
Beihai Park··································102

雍和宫
Yonghegong Lamasery·················114

前 言

中华人民共和国首都北京是一座世界历史文化名城。蓟、涿、幽州、南京、燕京、中都、大都、北平是它在各个历史时期的名称。过去的北京是一座四方城，城的周围围绕着高大坚固的砖砌城墙，城墙四面对称地开着十六个拱形门洞，门洞之上是飞檐凌空的城楼。如今，"城中之城"紫禁城仍然像一颗宝石闪烁在北京城的中央。

蓟是北京的乳名。公元前十一世纪，蓟国是统治中国北方的西周王朝的一个分封国。春秋（公元前七七零年——前四七六年）中期，位于蓟国西南面的另一个封国燕吞并了蓟，并迁都于蓟城。从这时起，直到公元前二二六年燕国被强大的秦国所灭之前，蓟城一直是燕的都城。当年的蓟城就在现在北京城区的西南部。

北京全市面积16807平方公里，人口1300多万。北京地处华北平原北端，西、北、东三面环山，东南为平原。古人曾以"北据居庸，西峙太行，东连山海，南俯中原"来形容北京地理位置的重要。北京北依山险，南控平原，是贯通中国东北、华北地区的交通要冲，所以它是历代兵家必争之地。

逝者留痕，在三千年的历史中，北京经历过苦难，有过屈辱，流过泪，滴过血，也迎来了辉煌。1949年10月1日，中华人民共和国成立，作为新生的共和国的首都，古城的历史揭开了新的一页。要想重新目睹北京旧时的风貌和曾有的历史场景已不可能，但历史的遗迹无时无刻不在告诉我们这里曾经有过的故事，有过的人。这里有世界上保存最完好、规模最宏大的宫殿建筑群——故宫，有风景绚丽、建筑辉煌的皇家园林——颐和园、北海，有设计巧妙、气势宏伟的坛庙——天坛，有工程浩大、蜿蜒万里的古代军事设施——长城，有藏传佛教格鲁派皇家寺院——雍和宫，还有布局严整、殿宇错落的帝王陵寝——明十三陵。北京的长城、故宫、颐和园、天坛、十三陵、周口店北京猿人遗址被联合国教科文组织列入《世界遗产名录》。一座默默耸立的古塔，往往凝聚着一代艺术的精华；一块苔藓斑驳的碑石，或许记载着轰动一时的壮举。北京就好象是一座壮美的历史博物馆，记录着古都的过去，迎接着美好的未来。

为了使读者更好地了解北京，我们编辑的这本图册，从北京大量的名胜古迹中精选了8个景点，希望通过对这8个景点的介绍，向读者展现古老而迷人的北京。

FOREWORD

Beijing, capital of the People's Republic of China, is a city of history and culture. In its time it has been known by the names Ji, Zhuo, Youzhou, Nanjing, Yanjing, Zhongdu, Dadu, and Beiping. The old city of Beijing was a quadrate enclosed by tall, solid walls in which sixteen arched gates, topped by towers with tilted eaves, were symmetrically arranged. The Forbidden City still stands at the center of Beijing today.

Ji is the name by which Beijing was first known. In the 11th century B.C. it was a vassal state of the Western Zhou Dynasty until annexed in the mid Spring and Autumn Period (770-476 B.C.) by another vassal state, Yan. The capital then moved to the city of Ji, where it remained until Yan was conquered by the State of Qin in 226 B.C. The site of the ancient city of Ji is believed to be in the southwestern suburbs of present-day Beijing.

Beijing covers an area of 16,807 square kilometers at the northern end of the North China Plains. It has a population of 13 million. To its west, north and east are mountain ranges, and to its southeast are flatlands. As once described in an ancient volume, "Beijing's head rests on the Juyong Pass; the Taihang Mountains rise to its west; to its east are mountains and the sea; and to its south it overlooks a plain." A strategic point linking northeastern and northern China, Beijing has throughout history been a focal point of military strategy.

During the past 3,000 years Beijing has known glory, tribulations and revival. On October 1, 1949, the People's Republic of China was founded, with Beijing as its capital. Although some of the city's old buildings have disappeared, Beijing's historical sites, reminiscent of people who lived here and events that occurred, remain. The capital's architectural monuments are, most famously, that colossal military installation the Great Wall; the Forbidden City, largest and best preserved imperial building complex in China; imperial resorts the Summer Palace and Beihai Park; the magnificent Temple of Heaven sacrificial compound; Yonghegong Lamasery, imperial temple of Tibetan Buddhism; and the Ming Tombs, where 13 Ming emperors are buried. Of these and Beijing's many other places of scenic and historic interest, the Great Wall, the Forbidden City, the Temple of Heaven, the Ming Tombs and the Peking man site at Zhoukoudian have been designated world cultural heritage.

This album looks at just eight of Beijing's scenic wonders.

天安门广场平面示意图
Map of Tian'anmen Square

天安门广场

　　在北京城中心是气势磅礴、雄伟壮丽的天安门广场。明清时，天安门广场被5米多高的宫墙围绕，它的东、西、南三面各建有一座3个卷洞的门，东面的叫"长安左门"，西面的叫"长安右门"，南面的叫"大明门"，形成一个封闭型的T字广场。广场上建有南北走向联檐通脊的朝房144间，称为"千步廊"。

　　新中国成立后，进行了两次扩展，如今的天安门广场北至金水桥，南达正阳门城楼下，东西两侧紧邻中国历史博物馆和人民大会堂。广场占地44万平方米，可容纳100万人集会，是目前世界上最大的城市中心广场。

TIAN'ANMEN SQUARE

　　Tian'anmen Square is at the center of Beijing. In the Ming and Qing dynasties it was enclosed by walls more than 5 meters high, in which were three gates. To the east was Chang'an Left Gate, to the west Chang'an Right Gate, and to the south Daming Gate. The square was in the shape of T at that time. A total of 144 courtier offices stretched from the south to the north in the square, whose eaves and ridges were jointed. It was called the "One Thousand Steps Corridor".

　　Since the People's Republic of China was founded in 1949, Tian'anmen Square has undergone two extensions. Today it links the Jinshui Bridge to the north and the Zhengyang (South-facing) Gate to the south. The Museum of Chinese History is on its east side, and the Great Hall of the People on its west. Occupying an area of 440,000 square meters, it is the largest downtown square in the world, and can hold one million people.

1. **天安门广场** 广场上建有人民英雄纪念碑和毛主席纪念堂。每天的升国旗仪式在广场举行。

1. Tian'anmen Square Site of the Monument to the People's Heroes, and the Memorial Hall of Chairman Mao Zedong, the flag-raising ceremony is held in the square every morning.

2. **华表** 在天安门前后，各有一对雕刻精美的汉白玉石华表，华表是重要建筑的装饰物。

2. **Huabiao** In front of and behind Tian'anmen stand a pair of exquisitely carved white marble Huabiao—a kind of ornamental stone column erected in front of palaces and tombs.

3. **正阳门** 是北京内城的正南门，过去专供皇帝出入。城楼建于1421年，高42米，位于全城的南北中轴线上。

3. **Zhengyang (South-facing) Gate** The southern front gate of the inner city of Beijing was for the exclusive use of emperors. Built in 1421, it is 42 meters high, and is on the north-to-south central axis of Beijing City.

4. **天安门城楼** 建在13米高的城台上，为歇山顶重檐式城楼。高33.7米，东西宽9间，进深5间，取"九五"之数，以示帝王尊严。过去，这里是封建王朝举行"颁诏"大典的地方。

4. Tian'anmen Gate Tower　Built on a 13-meter-high rostrum, the tower is 33.7 meters high, 9 bays wide from east to the west and 5 bays long. In feudal times this was where the Issuing-Edict Ceremony was held.

5. 天安门 原是明清皇城的正门，明永乐十五年（1417年）兴建，当时叫承天门，清顺治八年（1651年）重建后改称天安门。

5. Tian'anmen   During the Ming and Qing dynasties it was the front gate to the imperial palace. When first built in 1417 it was called Chengtianmen, and was renamed Tian'anmen after reconstruction in 1651.

故宫博物院平面示意图
Map of Forbidden City

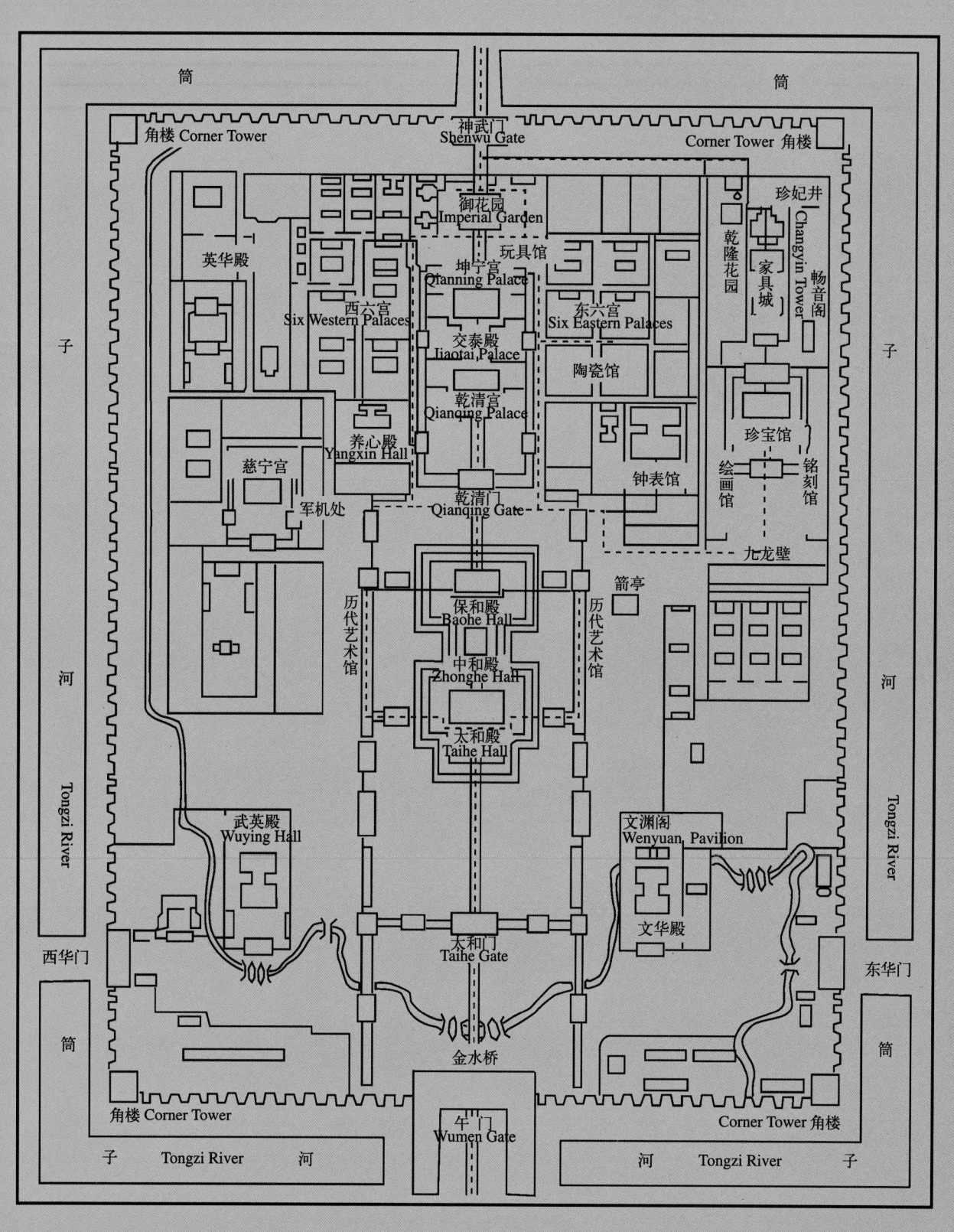

故　宫

　　故宫是明清两代的皇宫，旧称紫禁城，现名故宫博物院，是中国现存规模最大、最完整的古代宫殿建筑群。1987年，北京故宫被联合国教科文组织列入《世界遗产名录》。

　　故宫建于明永乐四年至十八年（1406-1420）。建筑规模宏大，总体布局严整，殿堂楼阁屋宇尽显皇家气派与帝王之尊。故宫占地72万平方米，宫室凡9900余间。四周有10米高的城墙，南北长960米，东西宽750米，墙外环绕着52米宽的护城河。

　　故宫分为外朝与内廷两大部分。南半部的外朝以太和、中和、保和三大殿为主体，两翼为文华、武英二殿。太和殿是皇帝举行盛大典礼的重要场所。北半部内廷以皇帝处理日常政务的乾清、交泰、坤宁三宫为中心，两侧有东、西六宫，是后、妃们生活居住的地方。明清两代共有24个皇帝在这里统治中国近500年。

　　故宫内收藏有自原始社会至清代的珍贵文物和艺术品达100万件，是研究和鉴赏中国文化艺术的宝库。

PALACE MUSEUM

　　Also known as the Forbidden City, the Palace Museum was the Imperial Palace of the Ming and Qing Dynasties. It is the largest and best-preserved imperial building complex extant in China. In 1987 it was designated world cultural heritage by UNESCO.

　　Built between 1406 and 1420, the palace occupies an area of 720,000 square meters, and has more than 9,900 rooms. Bounding the Palace Museum is a wall 10 meters tall that stretches 960 meters from north to south, and 750 meters from east to west. It is further bounded by a 50-meter-wide moat.

　　The Imperial Palace is divided into Outer and Inner Palaces. The Outer Palace in the south has three main buildings: Taihe (Supreme Harmony), Zhonghe (Middle Harmony) and Baohe (Preserving Harmony). These are flanked by the Wenhua (Literary Talent) and Wuying (Military Prowess) halls. Taihe Hall is where the emperor conducted grand ceremonies. The main structures in the Inner Palace are Qianqing (Heavenly Purity) Hall, Jiaotai (Harmonious Union) Hall and Kunning (Earthly Tranquility) Hall. The Eastern and Western palaces on the two sides were living quarters for imperial consorts. A total of 24 emperors from the Ming and Qing dynasties that ruled China for almost five centuries have lived in this palace.

　　The Palace Museum houses one million cultural relics and art masterpieces, dating from prehistory to the Qing Dynasty.

1. 故宫全景

1. The Imperial Palace

5. 鼎式炉 设在太和殿前的三层台面上，每层台面上都有6个形态精美的铜香炉，是在大典时熏香用的。三层台面上共有18个鼎式炉，象征清代的十八行省。

5. Tripod Censer There are six bronze censers on each tier of the three-tier terrace in front of Taihe Hall, symbolizing the 18 provinces of the Qing Dynasty. They were used to burn incense at grand ceremonies.

2. 太和殿 俗称金銮殿，建在有汉白玉围栏的三层高大露台上，殿高35米，建筑面积2377平方米，是中国最大的一座木结构宫殿。

2. Taihe (Supreme Harmony) Hall Popularly known as the Gold Throne Hall, Taihe stands on a white marble terrace of three tiers. At 35 meters in height and with a floorage of 2,377 square meters, it is the largest wood-structure hall in China.

3. 中和殿 内设宝座，皇帝参加大典前先在此休息，或由近臣演习礼仪。皇家九坛八庙每逢祭祀前一日，皇帝要来这里阅读祭文。

3. Zhonghe (Middle Harmony) Hall This is where the emperor rested and, from his throne, received greetings from officials before attending grand ceremonies. He also conducted ceremonial rites in the hall.

4. 保和殿 在清朝是宴请外藩王公大臣的场所，乾隆年间三年一次的殿试由太和殿移到这里举行。

4. Baohe (Preserving Harmony) Hall This is where the Qing emperor received foreign dukes, princes and ministers. During the reign of Emperor Qian Long the triennial imperial examination was also held here.

6. 日晷和嘉量 设在太和殿前露台东西两侧。日晷是中国古代的计时器，嘉量是古代的标准量器。日晷和嘉量并列陈设在宫殿前，表示天子有授时、授量之权，皇帝公正无私，皇权至高无上。

6. Sundial and Jialiang A sundial is an ancient timepiece, and the Jialiang an ancient measuring vessel. They stand on the two sides of the terrace in front of Taihe Hall, and signify the emperor's supreme authority.

7. 太和殿内景 殿内正中为雕有九条金龙的楠木宝座。明清时，当皇帝即位、生日、册立皇后、大将出征、金殿传胪及元旦、冬至时，在这里举行盛大典礼。

7. Inside Taihe Hall At the center of the hall is a gilded nanmu throne carved with nine dragons. During the Ming and Qing dynasties grand ceremonies were held here on such occasions as the emperor ascending the throne, the empress being selected, generals setting out on expeditions, successful imperial examination candidates being received, New Year's Day, the Winter Solstice and the emperor's birthday.

8. **宝座** 用楠木雕刻而成，上半部为圈椅状靠背，背上金龙缠绕，下部为金漆蟠龙须弥座，其高贵华美堪称故宫诸多宝座之魁首。宝座后是七扇金龙屏风。

8. **Imperial Throne** The throne is carved out of nanmu wood, with gilded coiled dragons forming its backrest and lower part. It is the most magnificent of all the thrones in the palace. Behind it stands a 7-leaf screen decorated with gold dragons.

9. 养心殿正殿 内设宝座、御案，皇帝在此办理日常政务及接见大臣等。

9. Yangxin (Mental Cultivation) Hall The emperor received officials from the throne and handled his daily work on the table in this hall.

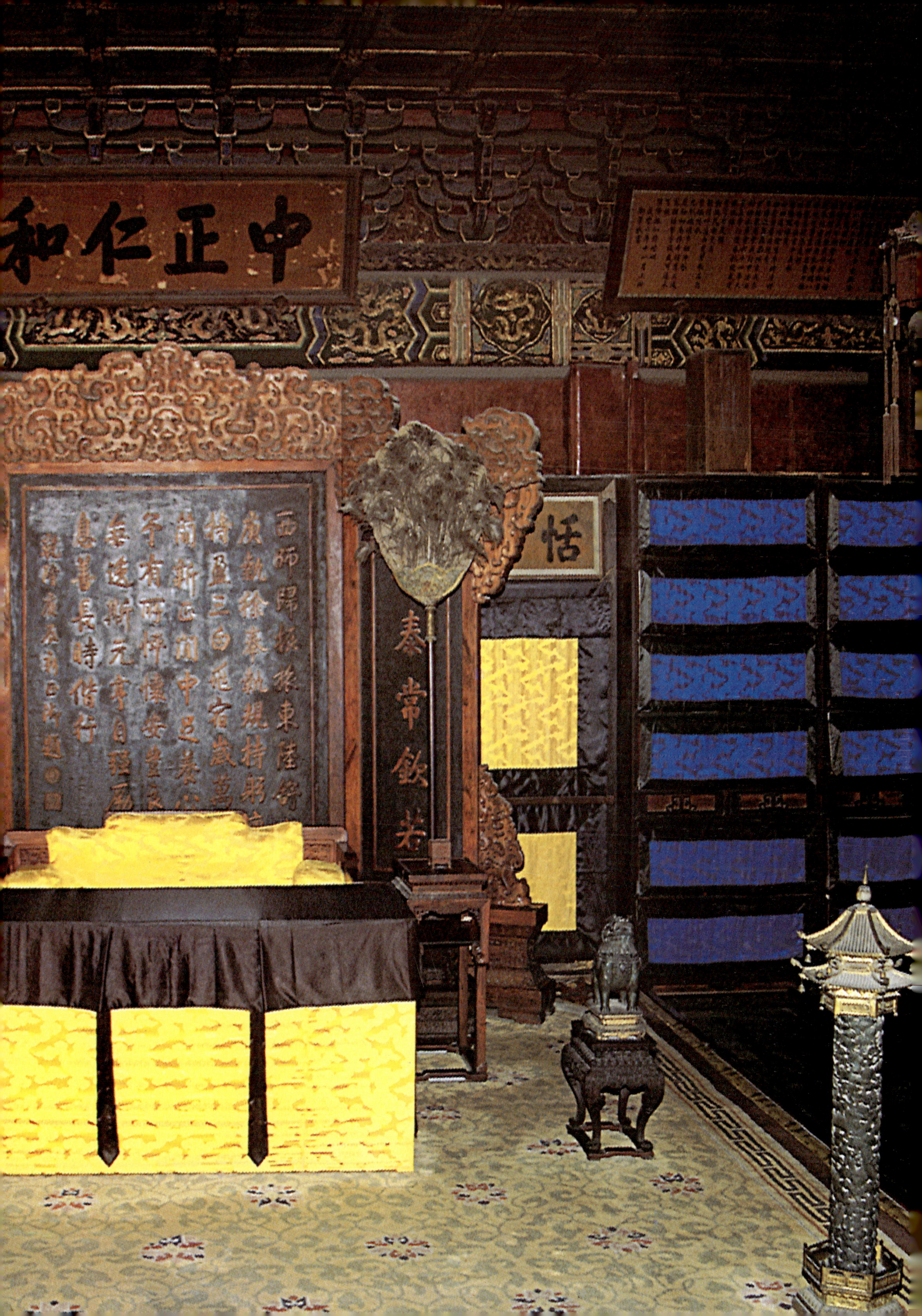
中正仁和
恬
奉常欽若

10. 养心殿东暖阁 1861年咸丰死后，慈禧太后在此实行"垂帘听政"48年。1912年2月12日，隆裕皇太后在这里公布了退位诏书，结束了清王朝的统治。

10. Eastern Warm Chamber of the Yangxin Hall On the death of Emperor Xian Feng in 1861, Empress Dowager Ci Xi ruled China for the following 48 years, from "behind the curtain." It was also here that the Empress Dowager Yu Long released the abdication edict on February 12, 1912, that marked the end of the Qing Dynasty.

11. 云龙陛石 在保和殿后面台阶的中央，斜放着一块汉白玉巨石，上刻九龙戏珠。陛石长16.57米，宽3.07米，厚1.7米，重250吨。

11. Cloud and Dragon Stone Carving Between the flights of steps in front of Baohe hall is a marble carving of nine dragons playing with pearls. The 250-ton slab is 16.57 meters long, 3.07 meters wide and 1.7 meters thick.

12. 雨花阁 建于乾隆十四年（1749年），为三明四暗的阁楼式建筑。它是故宫中的藏传佛教佛堂，也是故宫中唯一的藏式建筑。

12. Yuhua (Rain Flower) Tower Built in 1749, this was a hall of Tibetan Buddhism. It is the only Tibetan-style building in the Imperial Palace.

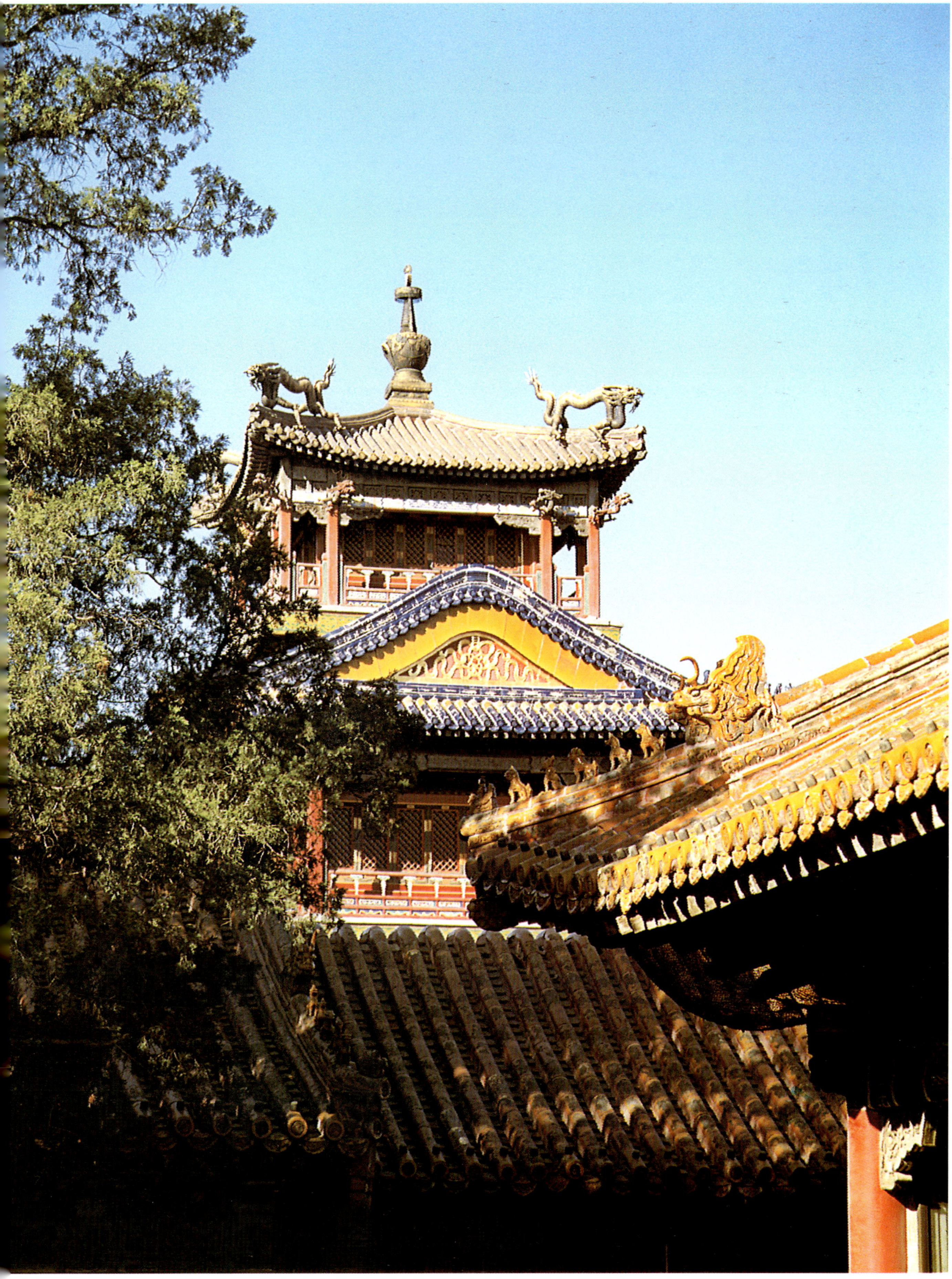

• 13

13. 乾清宫 是明末清初皇帝的寝宫和日常处理政务的重地。遇到节日，在这里大宴群臣。皇帝死了，灵柩暂停此宫。

13. Qianqing (Heavenly Purity) Hall   This was the living quarters of the emperor in the late Ming Dynasty and early years of the Qing Dynasty. He also did his daily work here. Banquets were held in the hall for court officials after grand ceremonies. On the emperor's demise, his coffin rested here for a time.

14. 镏金铜狮 乾清门前两侧的镏金铜狮，左雄右雌，铸造精致，形态威武，象征皇权的至高与威严。

14. Gilded Bronze Lions   The lions, one male and one female, guard either side of the Qianqing Gate. They are a symbol of the supreme authority of imperial power.

• 14

15. 乾清宫内景 乾清宫内"正大光明"匾的后面是清代存放秘密建储匣的地方。皇帝事先写好皇位继承人的名字，一式两份，一份存皇帝身边，一份封藏在建储匣内，皇帝死后由顾命大臣共同打开，宣布皇位继承人。

15. Inside Qianqing Hall   Above the throne is a horizontal plaque inscribed with the characters "Upright and Honest." During the Qing Dynasty the emperor wrote the name of his successor on two documents, one he kept himself, and the other was sealed in a box hidden behind this plaque. After the emperor passed away, the box would be opened under the supervision of specific officials who then officially announced the imperial successor.

• 15

26 Spectacular Scenic Sights of Beijing

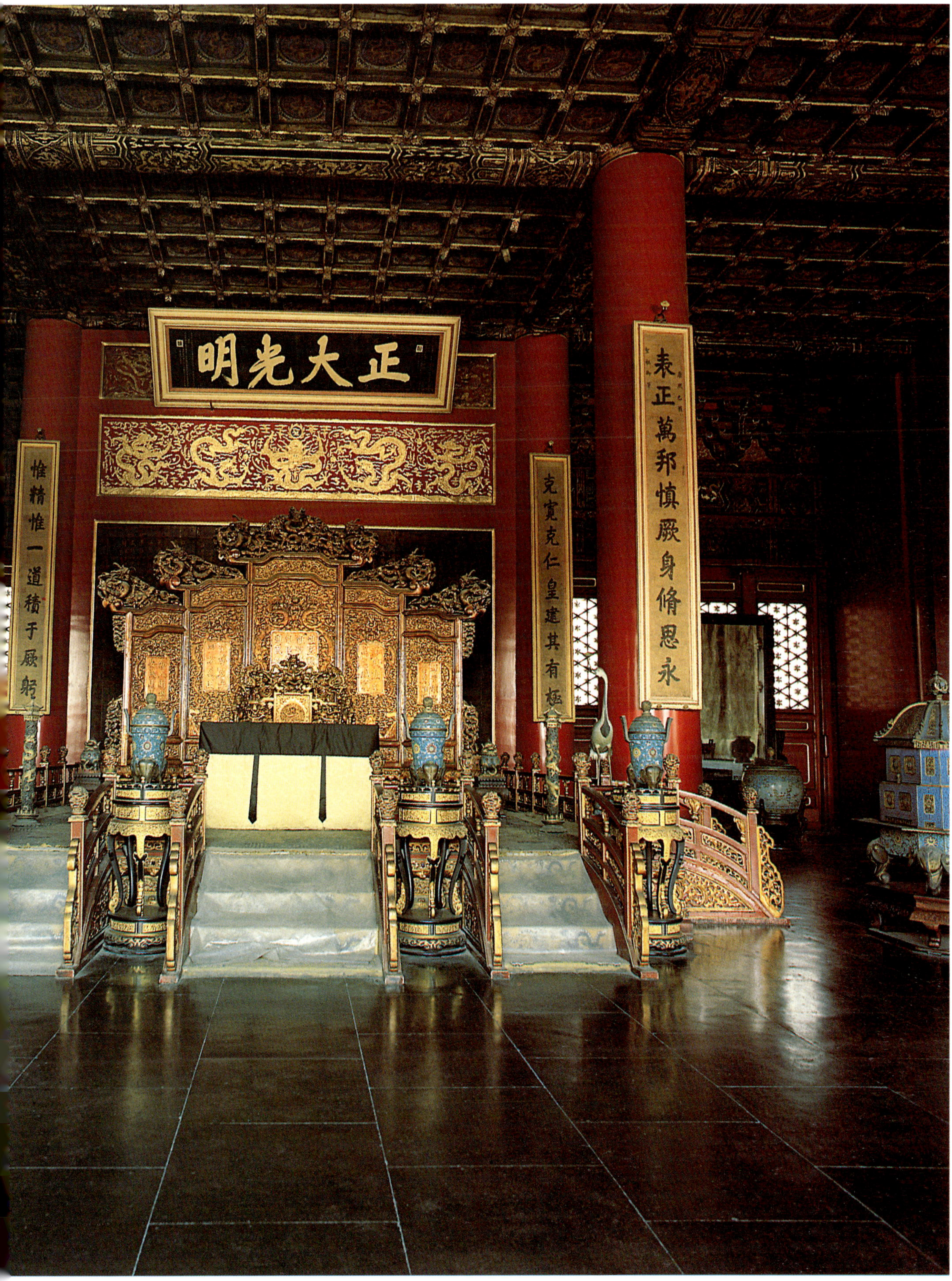
正大光明
表正萬邦慎厥身修思永
克寬克仁皇建其有極
惟精惟一道積于厥躬

16. 交泰殿 明清时为皇后举办寿庆活动的地方。1747年，乾隆将25颗代表皇权的宝玺藏于此殿。殿内东侧置铜壶滴漏一台，为中国古代记时器，西侧立大自鸣钟一座。

16. Jiaotai (Union) Hall During the Ming and Qing dynasties this hall was where the empress' birthday was celebrated. In 1747 Emperor Qian Long hid 25 imperial seals here. By the eastern wall of the hall is a copper clepsydra, and by the western wall stands a big striking clock.

17. 储秀宫 面阔5间，是明、清两代后妃居住的寝宫。
17. Chuxiu (Gathering Elegance) Hall This was the living quarters for imperial consorts of the Ming and Qing dynasties.

18. 储秀宫东暖阁 始建于明永乐年间，清慈禧太后曾在这里住过。
18. Eastern Warm Chamber of the Chuxiu (Gathering Elegance) Hall It was built in the 15th century. Empress Dowager Ci Xi had ever lived here.

19. 龙凤喜床 雕刻精美华贵，床上置明黄缎彩绣百子被，挂五彩纳纱百子帐。

19. Imperial Wedding Bed The bed is ornately carved. On it are bright yellow quilts of silk and satin embroidered with the 100 Boy Pattern. A gauze curtain, also bearing the pattern, hangs from it.

20. 坤宁宫皇帝大婚洞房 明朝时坤宁宫是皇后的寝宫，清初重建后将西暖阁改为祭神的场所，东暖阁则作为皇帝结婚的洞房。婚后第三天，皇帝、皇后便回各自的住所。

20. Imperial Bridal Chamber in Kunning (Earthly Tranquility) Hall Kunning Hall was the living quarters of the empress during the Ming Dynasty. After reconstruction during the Qing Dynasty, its Western Warm Chamber became a sacrificial hall, and the Eastern Warm Chamber served as the imperial bridal chamber. The emperor and empress returned to their respective living quarters three days after the wedding.

· 21

21. 五彩纳纱百子帐 图案优美，绣工精细，一百个儿童个个神态自然，富有童趣。百子帐象征着皇帝"子孙万代"、"多福多寿"。

21. Bed Curtain in the 100-Boy Pattern The curtain is embroidered with 100 charming boys of various facial expressions and indicates felicity and longevity.

· 22

22. **畅音阁** 故宫有大小戏台七、八座，畅音阁是其中最大的一座。

22. **Changying (Smooth Music) Tower** There are a total of eight opera towers in the Imperial Palace. This is the largest.

23. **角楼** 建于宫墙四角顶端，结构复杂，造型奇特，精美绝伦，是中国民族建筑艺术的杰作之一。

23. **Corner Tower** There is a tower at each of the four corners of the palace wall, each of a complex structure and exotic shape.

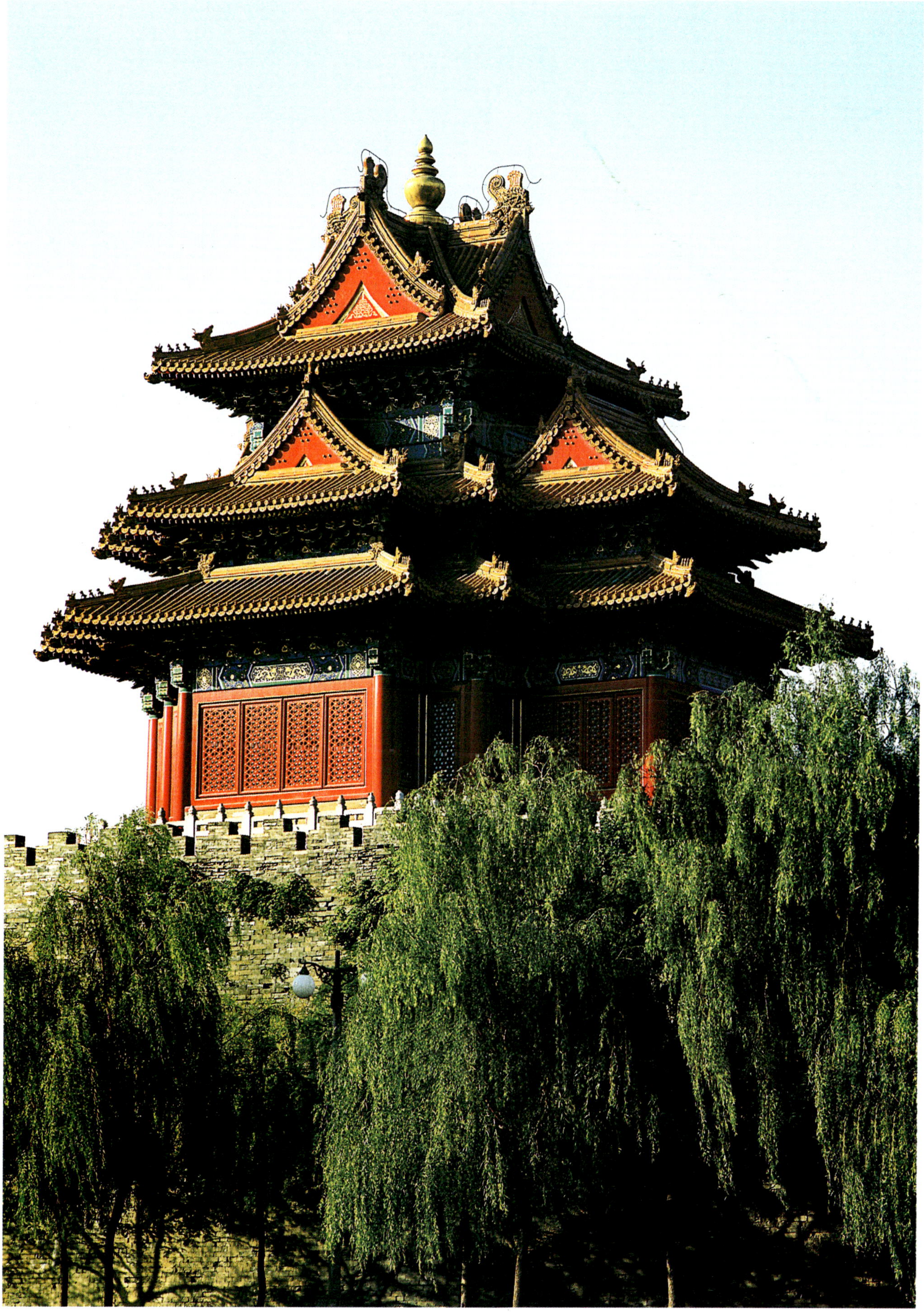

· 23

24. 万春亭 位于御花园东半部，方形重檐，伞状攒尖圆顶，下檐四角各出三支飞檐，美观大方，与园内西半部的千秋亭相对应。

24. Wanchun (Ten Thousand Spring) Pavilion The pavilion in the eastern part of the Imperial Garden has square multiple-tier eaves and an umbrella-shaped roof. It looks to the Qianqiu (Thousand Autumn) Pavilion at the other end of the garden.

25. 连理树 天一门内两棵交叉似"人"字形的柏树。传说一对夫妻死后化为两棵树，相交结合在一起。这两棵树被后人称为连理树，比喻夫妻间忠贞的爱情。

25. Twin Cypress Trees These two trees resemble, with their entwining branches, the Chinese character" 人 ". According to legend, they were once a devoted couple that became trees on their death, and remained entwined together. The trees are a symbol of conjugal loyalty and love.

26. 木化石盆景　这是一段十分珍贵奇特的木化石，石上刻有乾隆皇帝的题词。
26. Wood fossil bonsai　The rare fossil bears inscription of Qing Emperor Qian Long

27. 石子路的牡丹凤凰图案　园内道路用精选的各色鹅卵石镶成民间传说或戏曲故事、花卉等图案。牡丹凤凰寓意富贵吉祥。
27. Cobbled road of phoenix and peony design　Cobbled roads in the park are of various designs. The Phoenix and peony pattern symbolizes prosperity and good luck.

·26

·27

28. 钦安殿 御花园内的主体建筑。明清时，该殿是帝后供奉道教真武大帝的地方。

28. Qin'an (Imperial Peace) Hall This is the main building in the Imperial Garden, where the Taoist God Zhenwu (Perfected Warrior) was worshiped.

29. 钦安殿内景 殿内供奉道教水神真武大帝，每年立春、立夏、立秋、立冬等节令，皇帝到此拈香行礼，祈水神保皇宫、消火灾。

29. Inside Qin'an Hall Within a niche is the statue of Taoist God Zhenwu, worshiped as the god of water. At the beginning of each season, the emperor would come here and pray to Zhenwu for protection of the palace against fire.

30. **堆秀山御景亭**　堆秀山是用太湖石砌成的假山，山顶上高耸的亭子称御景亭，是帝后登高远望赏景之处。

30. **Yujing (Imperial Sight) Pavilion**　Standing on the Duixiu Hill rockery, this pavilion is where the emperor and empress viewed scenery within and outside the Imperial Palace.

天坛平面示意图
Map of Temple of Heaven

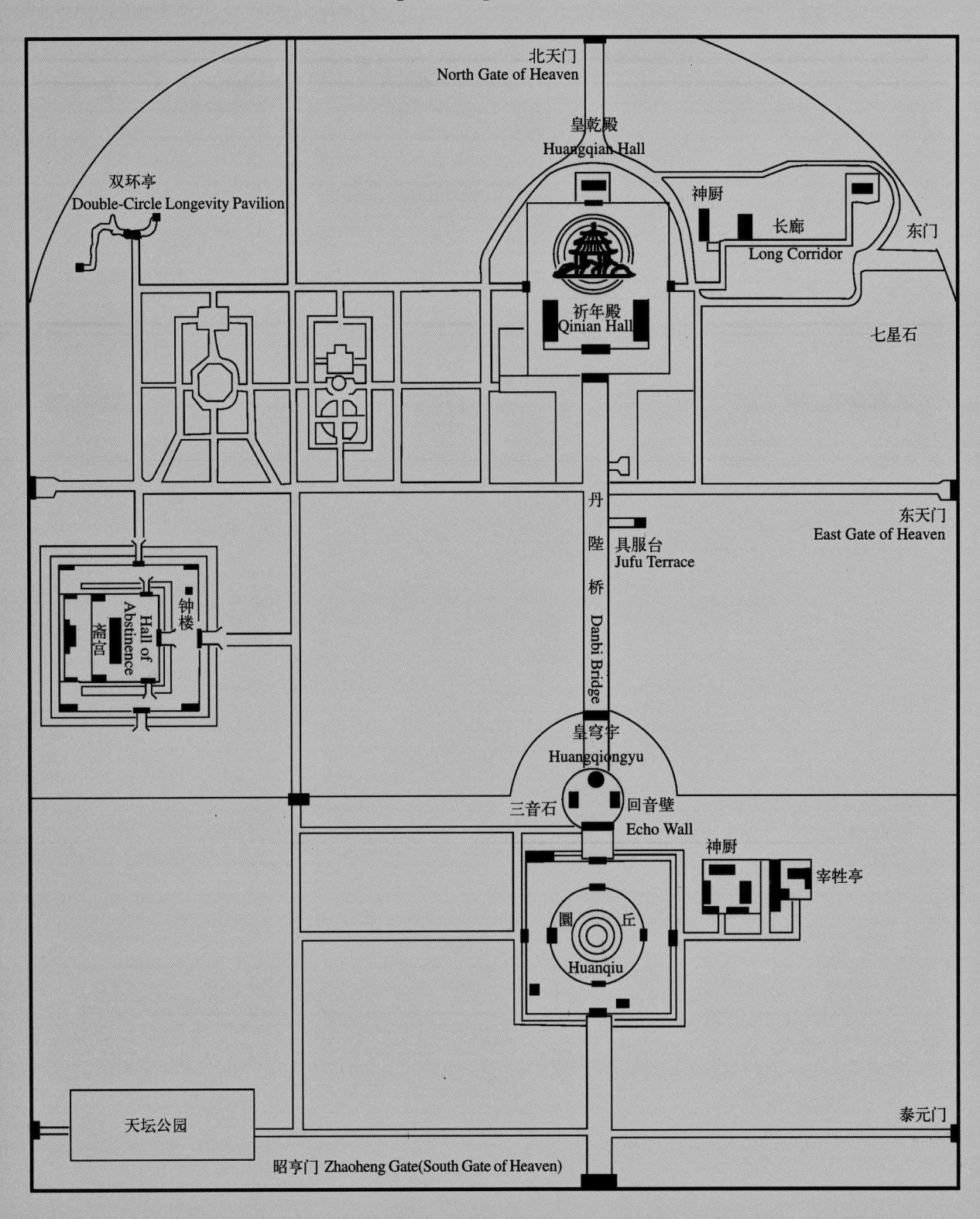

北天门 North Gate of Heaven

皇乾殿 Huangqian Hall

双环亭 Double-Circle Longevity Pavilion

神厨

长廊 Long Corridor

东门

祈年殿 Qinian Hall

七星石

丹陛桥 Danbi Bridge

具服台 Jufu Terrace

东天门 East Gate of Heaven

斋宫 Hall of Abstinence

钟楼

皇穹宇 Huangqiongyu

三音石 回音壁 Echo Wall

神厨 宰牲亭

圜丘 Huanqiu

天坛公园

泰元门

昭亨门 Zhaoheng Gate (South Gate of Heaven)

天　坛

　　天坛位于北京正阳门外东侧，是明清两朝皇帝祭天和祈谷的地方，也是世界上保存最完整的古代祭天建筑群。1998年，北京天坛被联合国教科文组织列入《世界遗产名录》。

　　天坛始建于明永乐十八年（1420年），以后又进行了增建和改建。天坛四周筑坛墙两道，北呈圆形，南为方形，以象征"天圆地方"，俗称"天地墙"。两道坛墙把全坛分为内坛和外坛两部分，总面积273公顷。内坛北为祈谷坛，南为圜丘坛，中间由丹陛桥相连，主要建筑分布于中轴线附近。西天门内建有斋宫，供帝王祀前斋戒居住。外坛西部设"神乐署"，掌管祭祀乐舞的演习和演奏。

　　天坛的主要建筑有祈年殿、皇穹宇、皇乾殿、圜丘、斋宫、长廊和双环万寿亭，还有回音壁、三音石和七星石等名胜古迹。

THE TEMPLE OF HEAVEN

　　East of Zhengyang Gate, the Temple of Heaven is where Ming and Qing emperors paid homage to the gods, made sacrifices and prayed for good harvests. The best-preserved sacrificial complex in the world, it was designated UNESCO world cultural heritage in 1998.

　　The temple was first built in 1420 during the Ming Dynasty. It has since undergone several extensions and reconstruction. Two walls divide it into an inner and outer temple. The northern part of the inner temple is semicircular, and the southern part is square. This indicates the ancient Chinese belief that heaven is round and that the earth is rectangular. Its total area is 273 hectares. The Qigu (Prayer for Grain) Terrace is at the northern end and the Huanqiu (Circular Mound) Alter at the southern end of the inner part of the complex. The Danbi Bridge links them. The temple's main structures are on a north-south axis. Inside Xitianmen (West Gate of Heaven) is the Palace of Abstinence, where the emperor fasted and bathed before the ceremony of offering sacrifices to heaven. At the western end of the outer part of the complex is the Shenyue (Heavenly Music) Hall where sacrificial music was rehearsed and performed.

　　The Temple of Heaven complex consists of the Hall of Prayer for Good Harvests, the Imperial Vault of Heaven, the Circular Mound Alter, the Palace of Abstinence, the Long Corridor and the Double-circle Longevity Pavilion. Other features are the Echo Wall, the Three-echo Stone and the Seven-star Stone.

1. **天坛全景** 俯瞰天坛主体建筑群，由南向北排列，宏伟壮观，气氛肃穆。

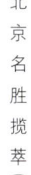

1. **Temple of Heaven**   The main structures of the Temple of Heaven stand from the south to the north.

2. 祈年殿 是皇帝祈谷的地方。殿高32米，直径24.2米。伞状镏金宝顶、三层重檐圆形的大殿，象征天圆；蓝色瓦顶象征蓝天。

2. Qinian (Prayer for Good Harvests) Hall This 32-meter-high and 24.2-meter-diameter hall is where the emperor prayed for good harvests. The blue tiles on its three-tier umbrella-shaped roof symbolize the blue sky, and the hall is round in tribute to heaven.

3. 祈谷坛 位于内坛北半部中央，为三层圆形石台，台面墁嵌清水澄浆方砖，俗称"金砖"，坛上中央为祈年殿。

3. Qigu (Prayer for Grain) Terrace This round terrace is at the center of the inner northern section of the complex. It is in three tiers, paved with square slabs. On top of the terrace, at its center, is Qinian Hall.

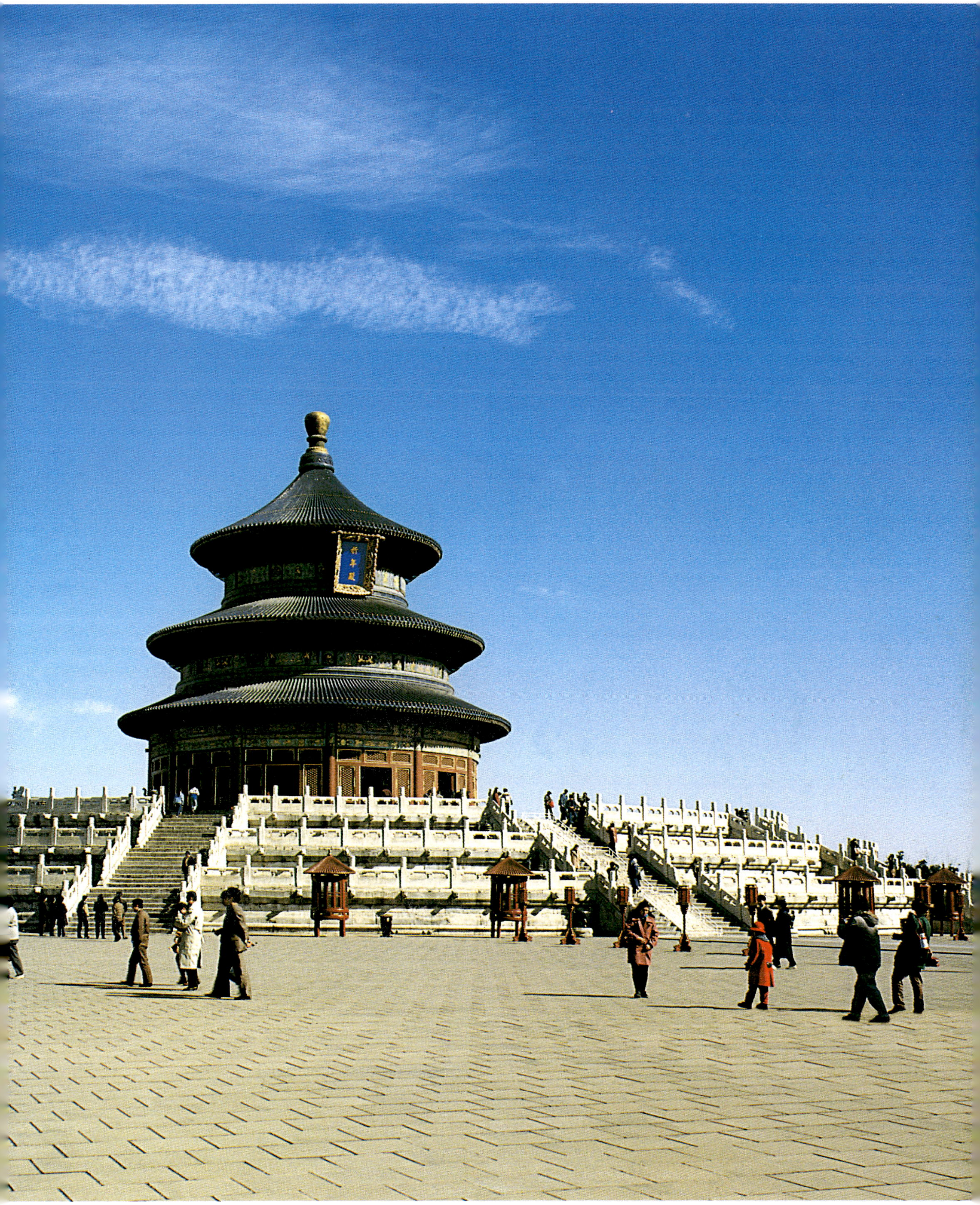

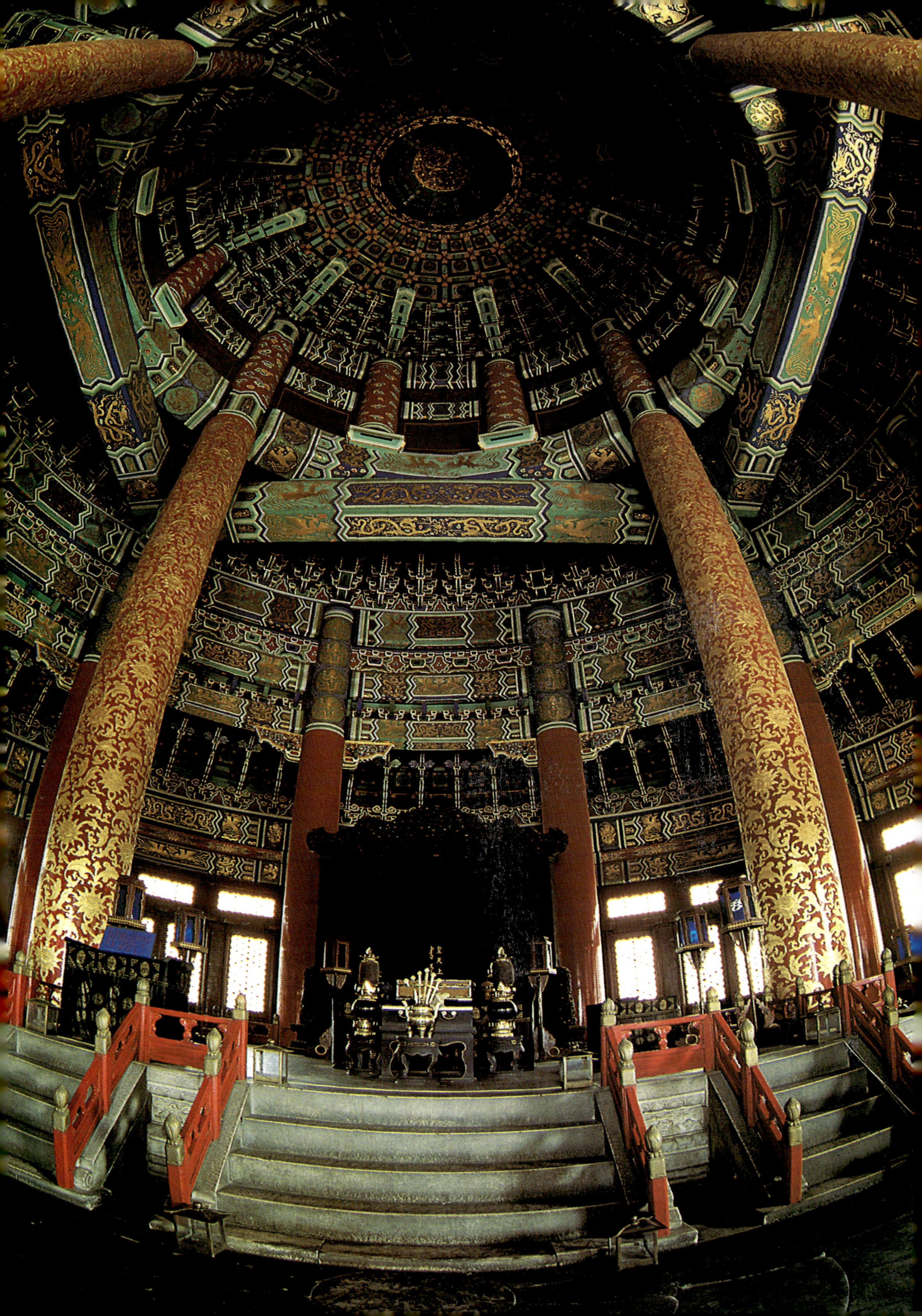

4. 祈年殿内景　殿内梁枋和天花均绘有龙凤合玺彩画，装饰精美，金碧辉煌。大殿全部采用木结构，28棵大柱支撑着整个殿顶的重量。据说大柱的数目是按天象所建。中间的4根大柱叫"通天柱"，象征春夏秋冬4个季节；中层12根大柱象征一年12个月；外层12根大柱象征一天12个时辰；中外层大柱相加24根象征一年24个节令；殿内全部28根大柱象征28星宿。宝顶下的雷公柱象征皇帝"一统天下"。

4. **Inside Qinian Hall**　The hall is constructed entirely of wood. Its ceiling and beans are painted in an exquisite design of dragons and phoenixes. Its roof is supported by 28 huge columns. The four central columns represent the four seasons of the year. They are surrounded by two rings, one inside the other, of 12 columns each. The inner ring symbolizes the 12 months of the year, and the outer, the 12 divisions of day and night. The pillars in the inner and outer circles stand for the 24 solar terms of the year, and the 28 pillars combined indicate the 28 constellations. The Leigong Pillar supporting the center of the ceiling symbolizes the absolute power of the emperor.

5. 皇天上帝神位　祈年殿内北部圆形石台上的雕龙宝座和东西两侧石台上的宝座分别供奉有皇天上帝神牌和皇帝祖先神牌，宝座后都有木质浮雕屏风。

5. **Memorial Tablet of the God of Heaven**　On a square stone platform in the northern end of the hall is a shrine decorated with dragon carvings on which the memorial tablet of the God of Heaven is kept. To its east and west on similar platforms are smaller shrines, in which are kept memorial tablets of imperial ancestors. Behind the shrines is a wooden relief screen.

6. 斋宫全景　古礼规定，皇帝祭天前三天须到斋宫斋戒。斋戒期间皇帝不如荤、不饮酒、不食葱蒜、不赏乐吊丧，也不理刑事等。祀日，皇帝从斋宫起驾登坛参礼祭天。
6. Palace of Abstinence　According to ancient protocols, the emperor came to the Palace of Abstinence three days before the annual sacrificial ceremony. There he abstained from meat, wine, garlic, shallots and music. He also refrained from dealing with any criminal affairs. On the day he was to pay homage to heaven, he left the palace for the sacrificial altar.

7. 敬天殿　斋宫的正殿，是皇帝祭祀前的斋戒处。
7. Jingtian (Paying Homage to Heaven) Hall　This is the main hall of the Palace of Abstinence.

8. 圜丘坛 是明清两朝皇帝每逢冬至日祭天的地方。坛外有两重围墙，第一重方形，第二重圆形，象征"天圆地方"。圜丘坛通高5米，分三层，每层周边的汉白玉栏杆都雕有精美的云龙图案。

8. Huanqiu (Circular Mound) Altar During the Ming and Qing dynasties the emperor came to this altar in early winter to pay homage to Heaven. It is enclosed by two walls. One is circular and one square, representing heaven and earth. The altar is 5 meters high and in three tiers, around each of which are white marble balustrades engraved with clouds and dragons.

9. **天心石** 圜丘坛上层的中心是一块圆形大理石,被称为"天心石",也叫"太极石"。如站在天心石中心说话或唱歌,自己会听到洪亮的回音,而站在天心石以外则无此感觉。

9. **Tianxin (Heart of Heaven) Stone** Also called the Taiji Stone, this is a round marble slab at the center of the top tier of the Circular Mound Altar. The voice of anyone standing on the stone as they speak or sing resonates echoes loudly.

10. **丹陛桥** 实为大道,因大道下有一隧道与道面立体交叉,故称桥。丹陛桥长360米,宽29.4米,宽阔平坦,连接圜丘坛与祈年殿。桥面中间为"神道",寓意升天之道;左为"御道",右为"王道"。祈谷祭天时,皇帝走御道,王公大臣走王道。桥体由南向北斜向升高,象征皇帝步步升高,可通达天庭。

10. **Danbi Bridge** This is actually a road 360 meters long and 29.4 meters wide that links Huanqiu Altar and Qinian Hall. It is called a bridge because of the tunnel beneath it. Its central path was reserved for gods, the left for the emperor, and that on the right for court officials. The bridge gradually ascends from south to north, thus taking the emperor nearer to heaven.

11. **长廊** 是祈谷坛的附属建筑。每逢祭祀日,大量的祭品就是通过长廊运送到祭坛的。长廊原建筑为前窗后墙、通脊连檐,共72间,所以也叫"七十二连房"。

11. **Long Corridor** This is annexed to the Qigu Terrace. At the time of the ceremony to pay homage to Heaven, sacrificial objects were taken to the terrace along this corridor. It has 72 sections. One side is open, and the other is walled.

· 9

· 10

· 11

· 13

48 Spectacular Scenic Sights of Beijing

12. 回音壁 环皇穹宇外的圆形围墙，高3.72米，厚0.9米，径61.5米，周长193.2米。墙壁由磨砖对缝砌成，弧度规则，墙面整齐光滑，具有很强的声波折射效果。

12. Echo Wall The circular wall surrounding the Imperial Vault of Heaven is 193.2 meters long, 3.72 meters high, 0.9 meters thick, and 61.5 meters in diameter. Its perfect radian and smooth surface of polished bricks enables it to refract wound waves.

13. 皇穹宇 是收藏神牌的地方。大殿外形优美，构筑别致；殿内为多层斗拱建筑结构，奇巧壮观。

13. Imperial Vault of Heaven In this were kept the wooden tablets of the gods. There are no beams in the vault roof; its support comes from numerous intertwined brackets.

· 12

14. 具服台 也叫更衣台。行"祈谷礼"大典前，在具服台上搭起一个方形黄缎子的临时幄帐，皇帝就是在这里换上蓝色祭服，礼毕返回这里更衣回宫。

14. Jufu (Dressing) Terrace This was also known as the Gengyi (Changing Clothes) Terrace when ceremonies paying homage to Heaven were held, a yellow satin tent was pitched on the terrace that the emperor used to change into the appropriate clothes for the ritual.

15. 皇乾殿 亦称"祈谷坛寝宫"，是尊藏"皇天上帝"及诸神神版的地方。这些神版平时供奉在皇乾殿中，只有举行祭天大典时才能请到圜丘坛受祭。

15. Huangqian Hall This is where memorial tablets of the God of Heaven and other gods, displayed on the Circular Mound Altar at sacrificial rites, were kept.

·14

·15

Spectacular Scenic Sights of Beijing

16. **九龙柏** 生长在回音壁西墙外，是一棵有500余年树龄的古柏。树体有九棵扭曲的树干紧紧盘绕在一起，形成一棵大树，故称"九龙柏"。

16. Nine-Dragon Cypress The tree outside the Echo Wall is more than 500 years old. Its twining branches resemble nine dragons.

17. **七星石** 位于长廊东面的旷地上。据说，明永乐帝建都北京时想寻找一祭天场所，一天夜里，他梦见天门大开，北斗七星落于此地，于是在此建天坛祀天。

17. Seven-Star Stones These are near the east entrance to the Long Corridor. It is said that Ming Emperor Yong Le once dreamt that the Gate of Heaven opened, and that the seven stars that made the Plough fell to earth. He built the Temple of Heaven on the spot where they landed.

18. **双环亭景区** 位于祈谷坛以西。景区内有"双环万寿亭"、"万胜亭"、"扇面亭"和六角形的"百花亭"。

18. Double-Circle Longevity Pavilion This is west of the Qigu Terrace. In its vicinity are the Wansheng Pavilion, Shanmian Pavilion and hexagonal Baihua Pavilion.

Spectacular Scenic Sights of Beijing

颐和园平面示意图
Map of Summer Palace

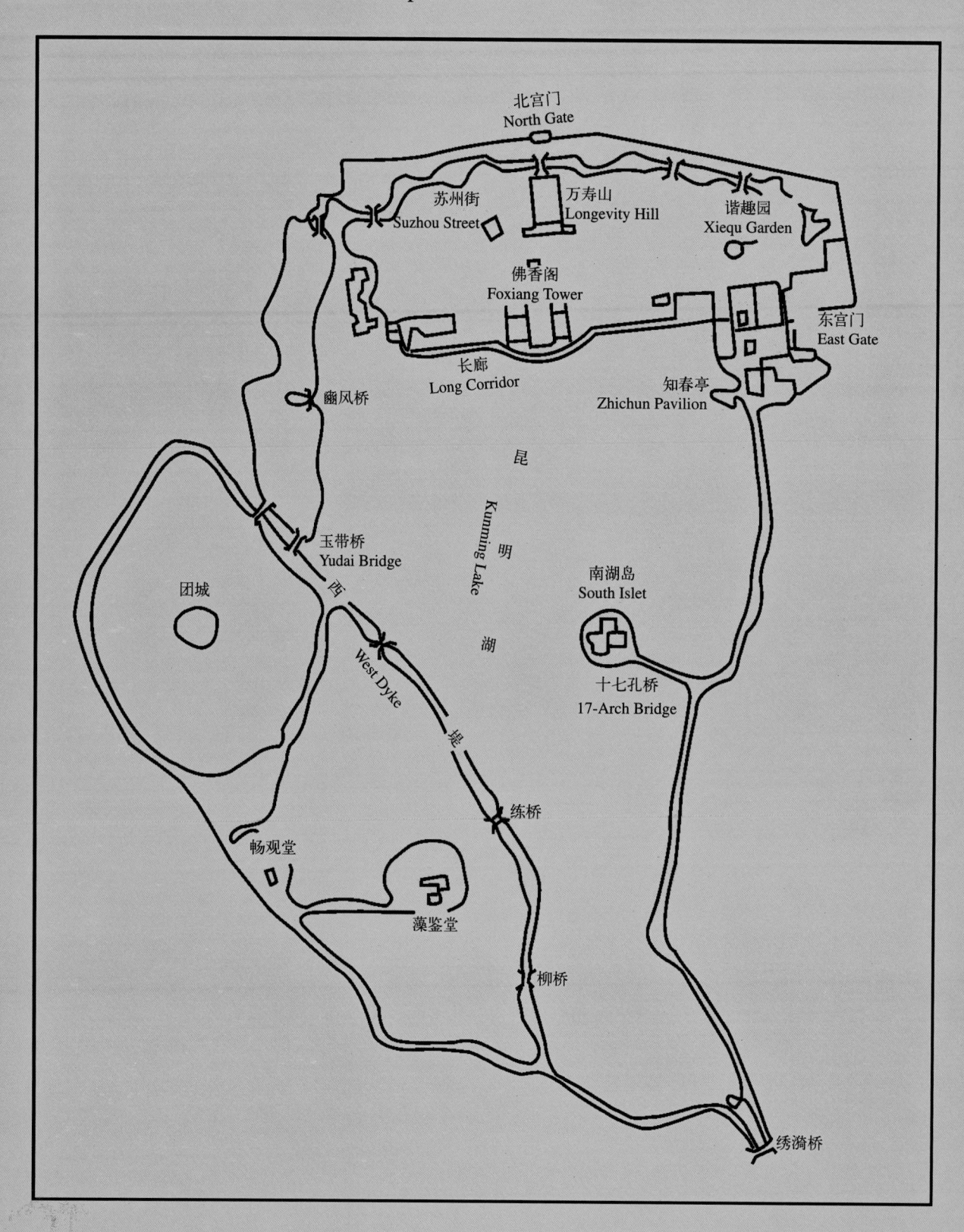

颐和园

　　颐和园位于北京西北郊，是中国现有规模最大、保存最完整的皇家园林和行宫。1998年，颐和园被联合国教科文组织列入《世界遗产名录》。1750年乾隆皇帝以庆贺皇太后60寿辰为名修建了清漪园，历时15年。1886年为庆贺慈禧太后50寿辰重修清漪园，改名为颐和园，作为慈禧太后的颐养之所。

　　颐和园主要由万寿山和昆明湖组成。全园占地面积290公顷，其中水面约220公顷，园内各种建筑3000余间。全园布局大体分为以仁寿殿为中心的政治活动区，以乐寿堂、玉澜堂、宜芸馆为主体的生活居住区和风景游览区三个主要区域，其中风景游览区是全园的精华。

　　颐和园游览区融山水、建筑、花木为一体。万寿山上的佛香阁是全园的建筑中心，金碧高耸；昆明湖水天空阔，旖旎动人；17孔桥宛若飞虹，跨向神山仙岛。后山后湖，宫阙巍峨，山水辉映。颐和园集传统造园艺术之大成，既有皇家园林恢弘富丽的气势，又充满了自然之趣。

THE SUMMER PALACE

　　Situated in Beijing's northwestern outskirts, the Summer Palace is China's largest and best-preserved imperial garden. In 1998 it was designated UNESCO world cultural heritage.

　　It was in 1750 that the Qingyi Garden, as it was originally known, was built at the behest of Emperor Qian Long to celebrate his mother's 60th birthday. Construction took 15 years. In 1886 the garden was refurbished to celebrate the 50th birthday of Empress Dowager Ci Xi, and its name was changed to the Summer Palace.

　　The Summer Palace is a 290-hector expanse with 220 hectors of waters, comprising Longevity Hill, the Kunming Lake, and more than 3,000 buildings. The garden has three main areas. That encompassing Renshou Hall area, where political matters were discussed; Leshou Hall, Yulan Hall and Yiyun Lodge, living quarters; and the scenic sight-seeing area.

　　The Summer Palace represents the cream of traditional gardening art. On Longevity Hill at the center of all other buildings is the imposing Foxiang Tower. Kunming Lake stretches out to meet the sky on the horizon, and the palace's 17-Arch Bridge links the South Islet and the bank of the lake like a rainbow.

1. 万寿山全景 以佛香阁为中心的主体建筑群气势恢弘，苍松翠柏中掩映着形式各异的殿、楼、亭、阁。山下沿湖岸建有728米的长廊。

1. Longevity Hill There are majestic buildings set off by lush trees on this hill, Foxiang Tower at their center. The Long Corridor is at its foot.

2. 东宫门　是颐和园的正门，设有 3 个门，两侧各有 1 个旁门，只有皇帝、皇太后进园时才全部打开，人们根据身份和官阶地位的不同，分别从 5 个门进园。
2. Eastern Palace Gate   This is the main entrance to the Summer Palace. It has three openings at the center and two side openings. These opened simultaneously only when emperors or empress dowagers arrived. Visitors came to the Summer Palace through entrances designated them according to their status and official rank.

3. 东宫门前的铜狮　一雄一雌，分列门前。雕铸精美，造型生动，花纹缜密，是清朝铜铸品中的上乘之作。
3. Bronze Lions   A pair of bronze lions, one male and one female, guards either side of the Eastern Palace Gate.

Spectacular Scenic Sights of Beijing

4. 玉澜堂 原为一组四通八达的穿堂殿，是光绪在园内的寝宫。戊戌（1898年）变法失败后，慈禧命人将院落封闭，幽禁光绪。

4. Yulan (Jade Ripples) Hall This was where Emperor Guang Xu resided at the Summer Palace. After the failure of the 1898 Reform Movement, Empress Dowager Ci Xi gave orders to seal off the courtyard and keep Emperor Guang Xu under house arrest.

5. 乐寿堂 是慈禧在颐和园内居住的寝宫。慈禧当政后期，许多重大决策都是在这里作出的。

5. Leshou (Happy Longevity) Hall This hall was where the Empress Dowager Ci Xi lived at the Summer Palace. During the latter years of her rule she made many crucial decisions here.

6. 仁寿殿 "仁寿"意即施仁政者可长寿。
6. Renshou (Benevolence and Longevity) Hall   The name of this hall indicates that benevolent rulers enjoy longevity.

7. 仁寿殿内景   慈禧、光绪在颐和园居住期间,临朝理政和朝会大臣的场所。殿内陈设显示了皇权的神圣和至高无上。
7. Inside Renshou Hall   This hall is where Empress Dowager Ci Xi and Emperor Guang Xu handled state affairs and gave audiences. Its décor and furnishings indicate the supreme authority of imperial power.

8. 水木自亲　是慈禧从水路到颐和园上下船的码头，也是乐寿堂前院的大门。门前两根高大立柱架起的半圆型铜圈，用于夜间挂灯照明。

8. Shuimuziqin (Water and Wood Are Friendly by Nature)　This is the port from where the Empress Dowager Ci Xi traveled by water to the Forbidden City. It was also the gate to the front courtyard of Leshou Hall. On its either side are high posts from which lamps were hung at night.

Spectacular Scenic Sights of Beijing

9. **德和园戏楼** 俗称大戏台，是一座高21米的三层戏楼，专供慈禧看戏的场所，被誉为"京剧的摇篮"。

9. **Grand Opera Tower in the Dehe Garden** This 21-meter-high tower is a three-story theater that was for the exclusive use of Empress Dowager Ci Xi. It is called the cradle of Peking Opera.

10. **玉带桥**　为西堤风格各异的六桥之一，因桥高且桥面薄，形状酷似玉带而得名。乾隆时期，玉带桥是连接清漪园和静明园水路交通的必经之地，为使帝后的大船能顺利通过，巧妙地建造了这座高拱位、造型优美的桥。
10. Yudai (Jade Ribbon) Bridge   This is one of the six bridges on the western shore. The name Jade Ribbon refers to its height, and to its slender deck.

11. **知春亭**　位于昆明湖东部水域中，是园内观赏湖山佳景的理想场所。
11. Zhichun (Be Aware of Spring) Pavilion   Standing on the eastern shore of Kunming Lake, this is the ideal spot from which to admire the hill and waters.

· 12

12. 昆明湖 万寿山脚下的昆明湖被几道湖堤分成 3 个主要水域，17 孔桥与南湖岛相连，湖堤沿岸建有楼、亭及形式多样的桥数座。

12. Kunming Lake At the foot of Longevity Hill, dykes divide Kunming Lake into three parts. The 17-Arch Bridge links Longevity Hill to the South Islet. Along its banks are towers, pavilions and bridges in various designs.

13. 十七孔桥 建于乾隆十五年（1750 年），东接东堤廊如亭，西连南湖岛，全长 150 多米，是中国皇家园林中现存最长的桥，因有 17 个桥券洞而得名。

13. 17-Arch Bridge Built in 1750, this bridge links the Kuoru Pavilion on the eastern shore to the lake's South Islet. Over 150 meters in length, it is the longest bridge extant in any of China's imperial gardens.

· 13

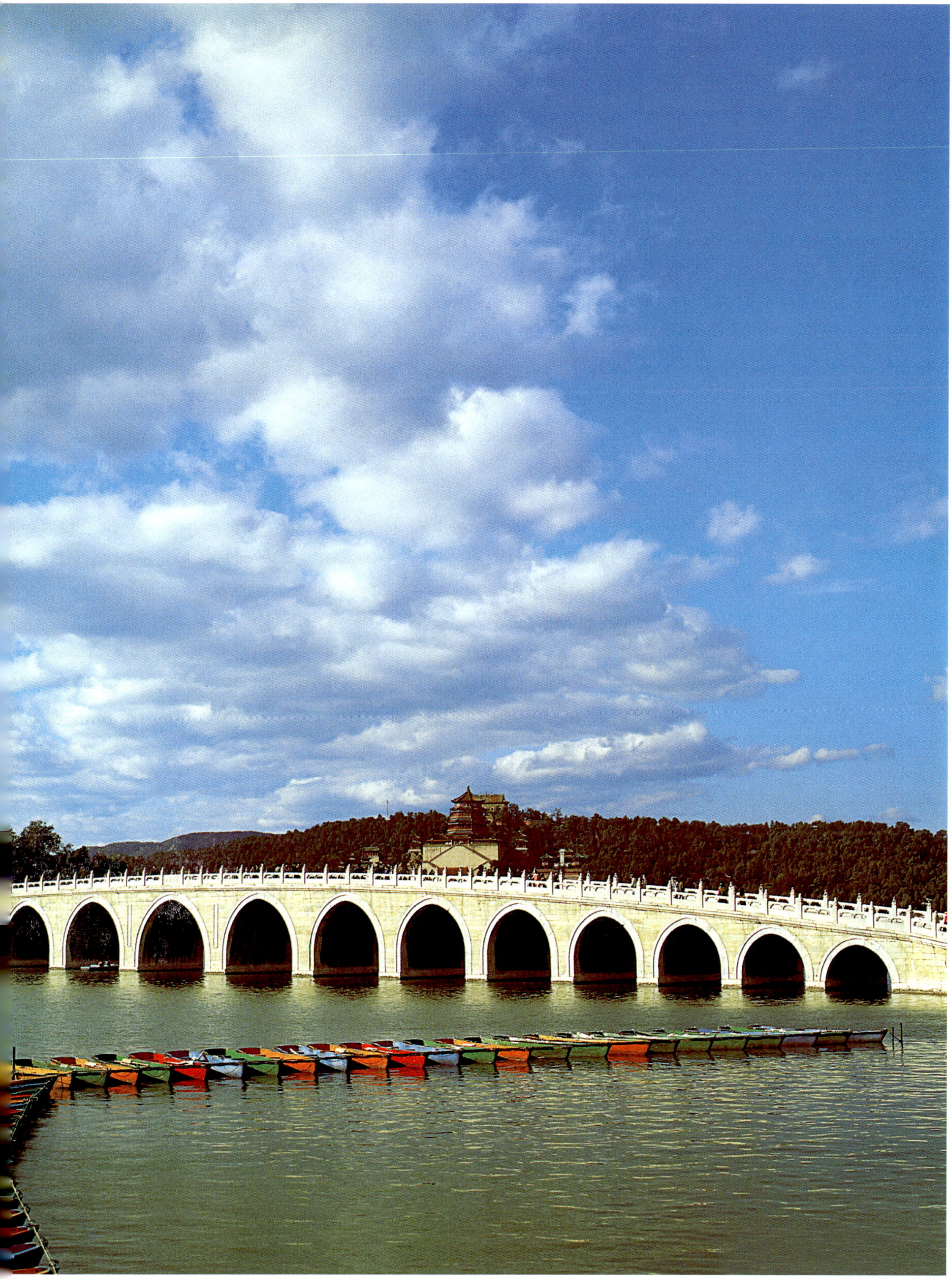

14. 清晏舫 俗称石舫，乾隆时修造，光绪时将船上建筑改为洋式舱楼，并在船体两侧各加1个机轮，形成西洋风格。船体用大块青石雕砌而成，长36米。

14. Qingyanfang   This 36–meter-long "stone boat", as it was known, was made out of huge stone blocks during the reign of Emperor Qian Long. During the reign of Emperor Guang Xu its cabin was transformed into a Western-style tower, and a wheel was added on each side.

15. 长廊 建于乾隆十五年（1750年），东起邀月门，西至石丈亭，全长728米，枋梁上绘有各种苏式彩画1万4千余幅，是中国古典园林中最长的游廊。

15. Long Corridor Built in 1750, the corridor stretches 728 meters from the Yaoyue Gate in the east to the Shizhang Pavilion in the west. Its interior is decorated with more than 14,000 colorful paintings. It is the longest corridor in any of China's traditional gardens.

· 15

16. 宝云阁 位于佛香阁西侧，俗称铜亭子，供喇嘛念经颂佛用。1755年铸造，高7.55米，重207吨，是中国铜亭建筑中最大、最精美的一座。

16. Baoyun (Precious Cloud) Tower Baoyun Tower, west of Foxiang Tower, popularly known as the Copper Pavilion, is where lamas chanted their prayers. Cast in 1755, it is 7.55 meters high, weighs 207 tons, and is the largest and most beautiful copper pavilion in China.

· 16

Spectacular Scenic Sights of Beijing

17. 佛香阁 佛香阁高41米，为八面三层四重檐的楼阁，气势雄伟壮观，它不仅是颐和园的标志，也是艺术价值很高的宗教建筑。"佛香"二字源自佛教对佛的歌颂。

17. Foxiang (Buddha Fragrance) Tower　This 41-meter-high octagonal tower is in three stories and has four tiers of eaves. It is the main landmark of the Summer Palace. Its name, Foxiang, constitutes a tribute to Buddha.

18. 智慧海 是一座两层的宗教建筑，全部用砖石发券砌成，没有一根梁、枋，俗称无梁殿。殿内供奉无量寿佛，又称"无量殿"。它的外墙壁上嵌有一排排精致的琉璃小佛像。

18. Zhihuihai (Sea of Wisdom)　This two-story religious stone and brick structure, free of beams or columns, is also called "No Beams Hall." Inside it is a statue of the Buddha of Infinite Life, and rows of small glazed Buddhas are inlaid in the external wall.

19. 万斤铜佛 是明朝弥陀寺内的一尊大铜佛，佛身高5米，重万斤，有12个头24只手，称千手千眼佛。

19. Bronze Buddha Statue Formerly housed in the Amitabha Temple of the Ming Dynasty, this statue is 5 meters high and weighs 5,000 kilograms. Its 12 heads and 24 hands have also given it the name "Buddha of 1,000 Eyes and 1,000 Hands."

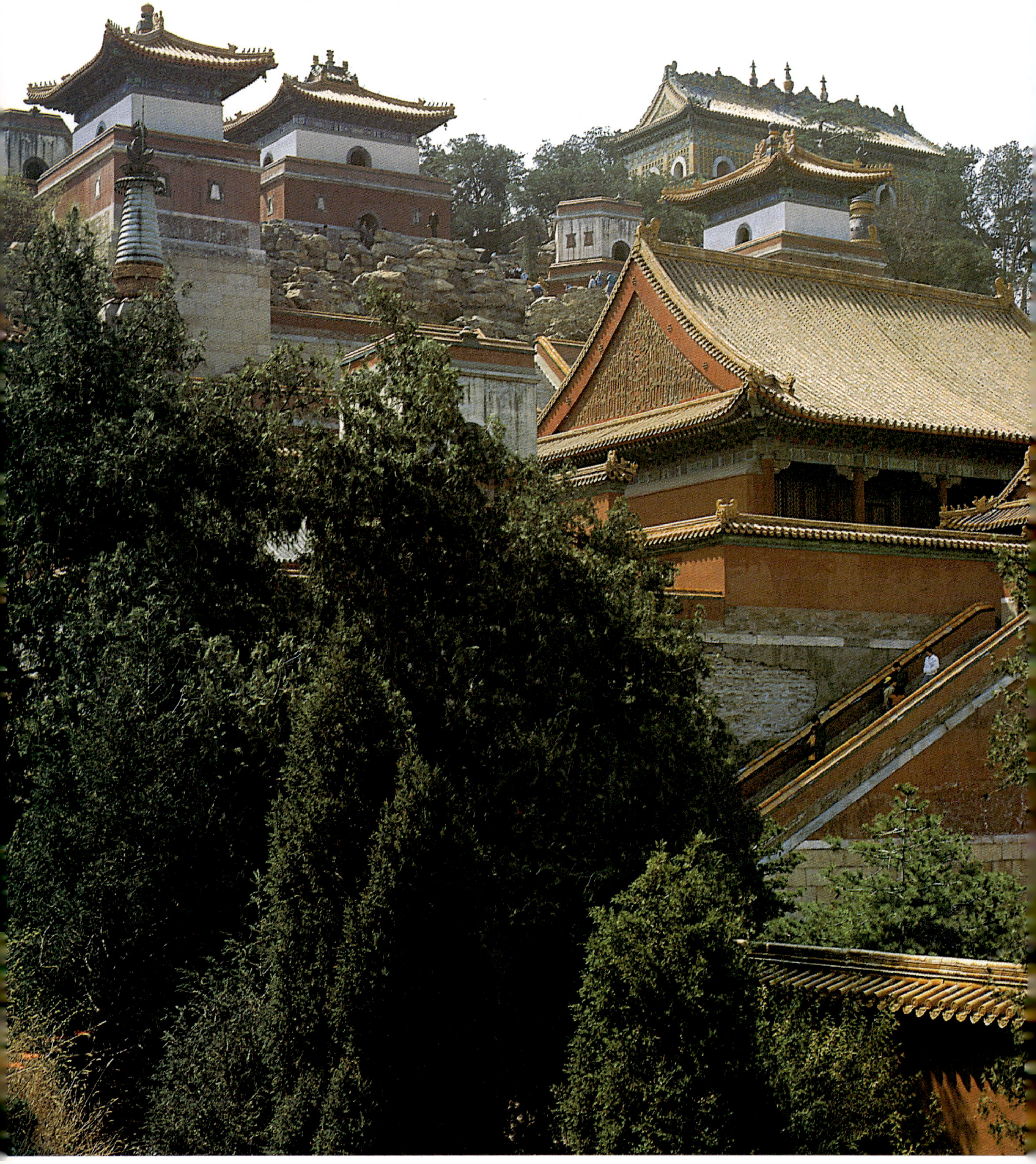

20. 四大部洲 是一组庞大的西藏桑鸢寺式的宗教建筑。"四大部洲"是佛教所称须弥山四方咸海中的四洲，即东胜神洲，男瞻部洲，西来货洲，北瞿卢洲。

20. Four Great Lands This colossal structure is in the style of the Samye Monastery in Tibet. The four great lands refer to the four continents in the oceans around the Mt. Sumeru, as described in Buddhist sutras.

21. 多宝琉璃塔 是后山东部半山处的一座佛塔，八面七级，高16米，塔身用五彩琉璃砖瓦和众多琉璃小佛像砌成，白色须弥座，顶上是镏金塔刹。

21. Multi-treasure Glazed Stupa Standing halfway up Rear Hill, this octahedral stupa is 16 meters high, in seven tiers. It is constructed from colorful glazed bricks and tiles, and ornamented with glazed Buddha figurines.

22. 知鱼桥 临塘而建，便于观看塘中鱼游乐。桥名源于中国古代哲学家庄子与惠子观鱼时的对话，即知鱼乐之桥。

22. Zhiyu (Knowing Fish) Bridge This bridge by the pool was for the specific purpose of viewing its fish. The name derives from a conversation between ancient Chinese philosophers Zhuangzi and Huizi. It means Know the Joy of Fish.

23. 谐趣园 素有"园中之园"的美称。园内中央是一个池塘，沿岸植柳，池中栽莲，亭、台、堂、榭围绕中央水池分布，由百间游廊和五座桥沟通，主体建筑涵远堂是慈禧游览休息的地方。池南岸有一座水榭，名为饮绿，是专供慈禧钓鱼的地方。东侧是知鱼桥，桥身低平，接近水面，便于观鱼，桥头建有牌坊，上有乾隆写的"知鱼桥"三字。

23. Xiequ (Harmonious Interest) Garden At the heart of the garden is a lotus pool, surrounded by willows, pavilions, halls and terraces. Corridors and five small bridges link these buildings. Its main structure, Hanyuan Hall, is where Empress Dowager Ci Xi rested while making a tour of the palace. On the southern bank of the pool is Yinlu (Drinking Green) Pavilion, where Ci Xi would fish. To its east is the low, flat Zhiyu (Knowing Fish) Bridge ideal for looking at the fish swimming in the pool. At its one end stands an Archway bearing Emperor Qian Long's personal inscription: Zhiyu Bridge.

· 24

24. 饮绿亭 临水而建，是慈禧在园内的垂钓处，两侧与沿池的曲廊相通。
24. Yinlu Pavilion   Sitting by the lake, the pavilion is the fishing place for Empress Dowager Ci Xi. It is joined with corridors on either side.

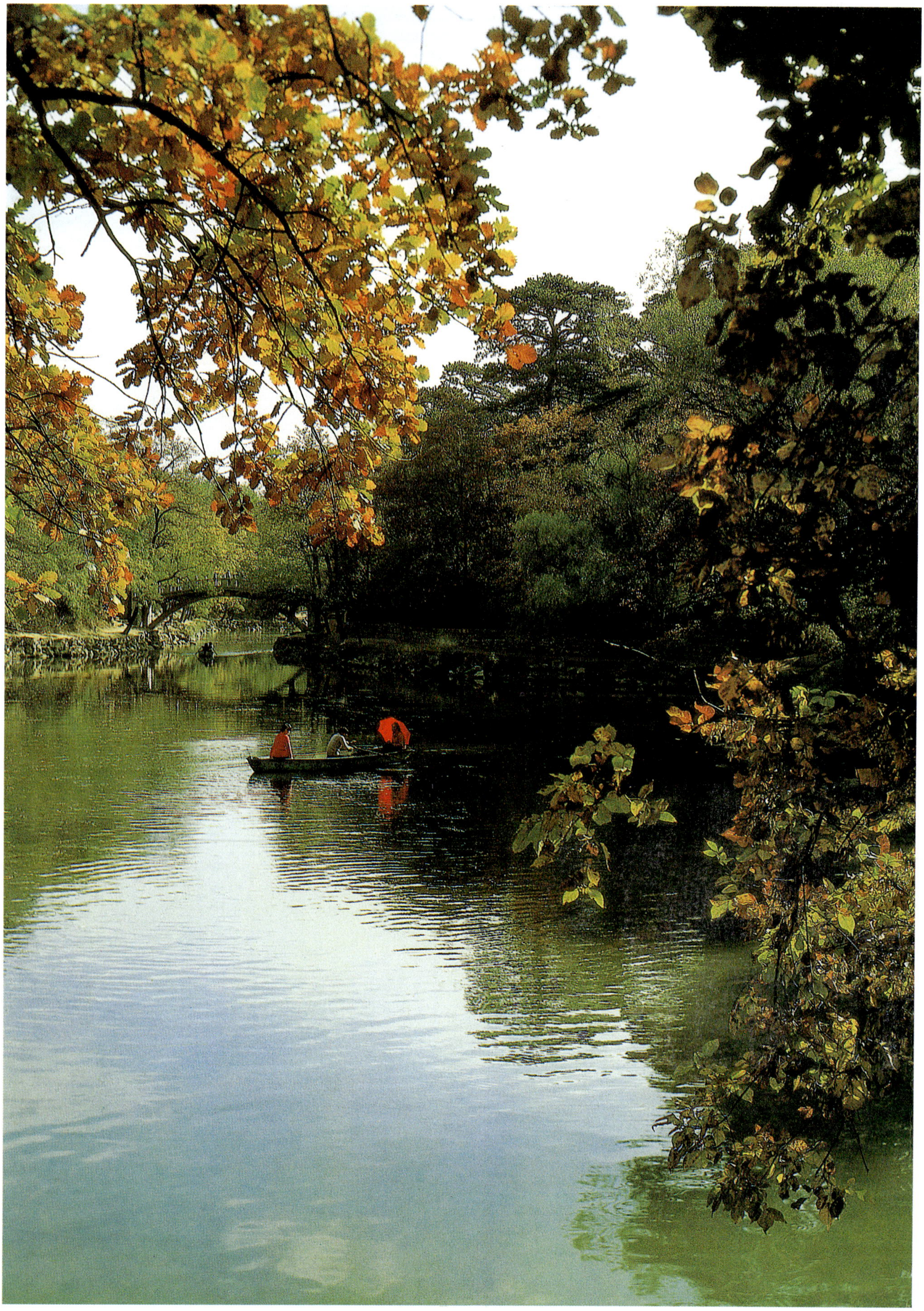

· 25

25. 后湖 是沿万寿山北麓仿江南景色开挖的人工河，亦称苏州河，全长约1000米。河上建有各式桥梁数座，两岸植花木，景色秀丽、宁静。

25. Rear Lake Stretching 1,000 meters along the northern slope of Longevity Hill, this is an artificial lake built in the style of the landscapes of southern China. It is also known as the Suzhou River. Over it are several bridges in various designs. Trees and flowers grow on its banks.

26. 苏州街 位于后湖中段，仿苏州水街修建，是一处既有江南韵味、又有北国风情的宫廷商肆。游人可兑换仿清制铜钱购买纪念品、风味小吃及品茶。

26. Suzhou Street A 300-meter course in the mid section of the Rear Lake, this is a replica of a river-side street in Suzhou, southern China. On this commercial street tourists can purchase imitation copper coins, the currency used in the Qing Dynasty, and use them to buy souvenirs, try local snacks, and drink tea.

八达岭长城平面示意图
Map of Badaling Great Wall

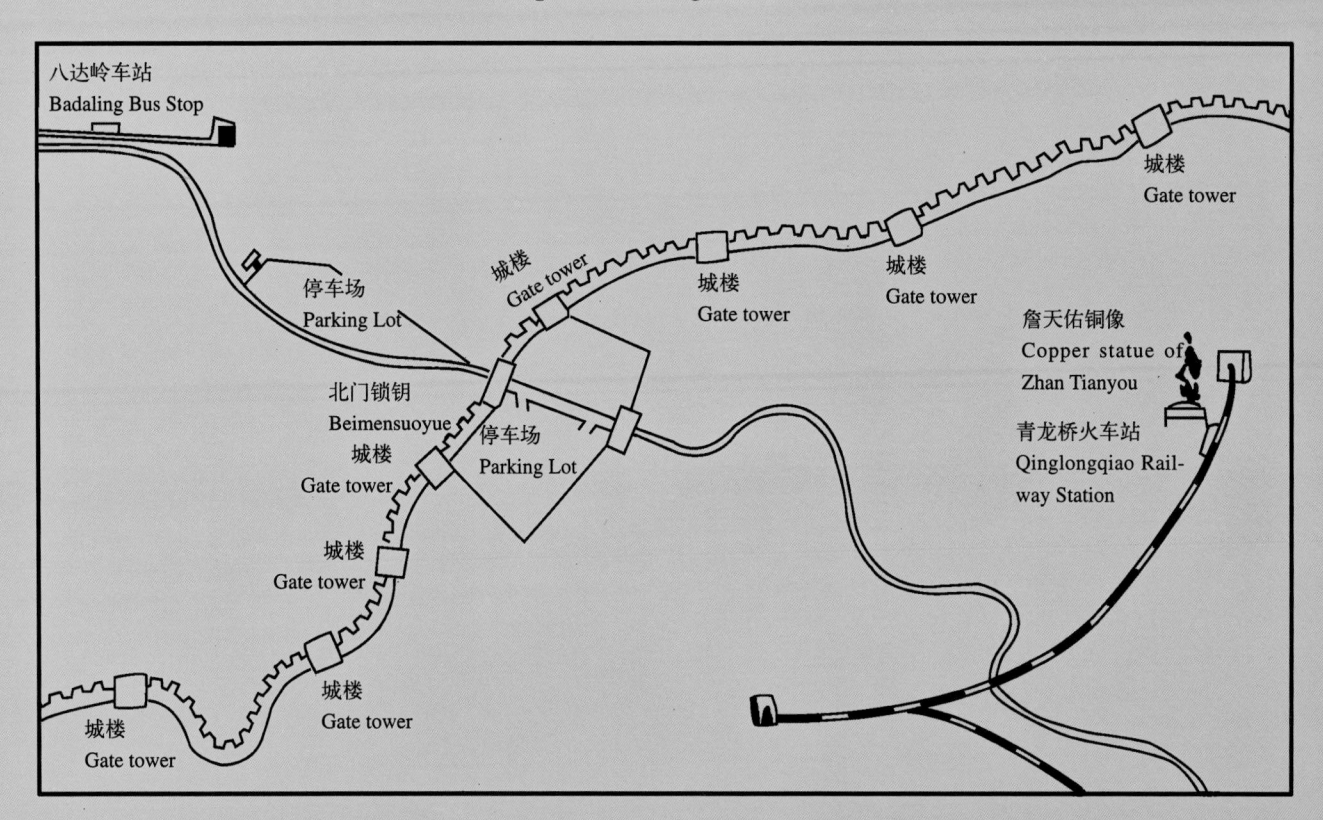

- 八达岭车站 Badaling Bus Stop
- 停车场 Parking Lot
- 城楼 Gate tower
- 北门锁钥 Beimensuoyue
- 停车场 Parking Lot
- 詹天佑铜像 Copper statue of Zhan Tianyou
- 青龙桥火车站 Qinglongqiao Railway Station

长　城

　　长城始建于公元前7世纪。秦始皇（嬴政）统一中国后，为防止北方匈奴南侵，用了十余年时间，将各诸侯国建造的长城进行大规模的修复、增筑和连接，形成了完整而庞大的军事防御体系——长城。以后历代王朝又进行了修补、完善和增筑。现在的长城遗迹大都保持着原貌，有的地段已经过整修复原。1987年长城被联合国教科文组织列入《世界遗产名录》。

　　长城西起甘肃省嘉峪关，东至河北省渤海沿岸的山海关，中间横跨六省一市，绵延6700公里。长城从中国的大西部，蜿蜒起伏，或直冲山巅，或横卧戈壁，或跨荒漠，或穿行于茫茫大草原，直达渤海海岸。

　　北京八达岭、金山岭、慕田峪等处的长城大都建在崇山峻岭之上，墙体沿着山脊把蜿蜒无尽的山势勾画出清晰的轮廓，城墙上建有无数坚实雄壮的敌台、敌楼，与矗立于崇山峻岭上的烽火台遥相呼应。

THE GREAT WALL

　　The Great Wall was designated world cultural heritage by UNESCO in 1987.

　　It was first built in the 7th century BC. On Emperor Qin Shihuang unifying China five centuries later, he got all the sections of wall in various states repaired and linked up, so as to build a colossal and complete defense system. The project took 10 years. The Great Wall has been reconstructed and expanded periodically in the centuries following. Today most of its sections, dotted with beacon towers and watchtowers, look as they originally did.

　　The Great Wall is 6,700 kilometers long, running from Jiayuguan Pass in Gansu Province in the west to the Shanghaiguan Pass, Hebei Province in the east. It traverses six provinces and one municipality, twisting over mountains, deserts and pastures towards the Bohai Sea shore.

　　Seen from a distance, the Beijing section is a winding trail over high mountain ranges.

1. 八达岭长城　位于北京城西北60公里处，建于明弘治十八年（1505年）。八达岭长城有东西两座关门，东叫"居庸外镇"，西称"北门锁钥"，关门城台南北两侧依山而筑，总长3720米。

1. **The Great Wall at Badaling** This section, 60 kilometers northwest of Beijing City, was built in 1505 during the Ming Dynasty. It stretches 3,720 meters along the mountain, and has two pass gates at the eastern and western ends.

2. 山海关 位于河北省秦皇岛市，是长城东部起点。明初置关戍守。山海关北依角山，南临渤海，形势险要，被称为"天下第一关"。

2. Shanhaiguan Pass Located in Qinhuangdao City, Hebei Province, this is the eastern end of the Great Wall. The pass was built and defended at the beginning of the Ming Dynasty. Its position at the foot of Jiaoshan Mountain, facing the Bohai Sea, makes it difficult to assail. It is therefore known as No.1 Majestic Pass on Earth.

3. 嘉峪关 位于甘肃省内嘉峪山东南麓，是长城西部终点，自古为东西交通要冲。

3. Jiayuguan Pass The western end of the Great Wall, it sits on the southeastern slope of the Jiayu Mountain in Gansu Province. It has been a strategic point of transportation since ancient time.

4. **幕田峪长城**　位于北京市怀柔区。这段长城始建于南北朝时期（479-502年），总长2250米，海拔535米。

4. **Mutianyu Great Wall**　Located in the Huairou District of Beijing, this section was first built during the Southern and Northern Dynasties (479-502). It is 2,250 meters long and 535 meters above sea level.

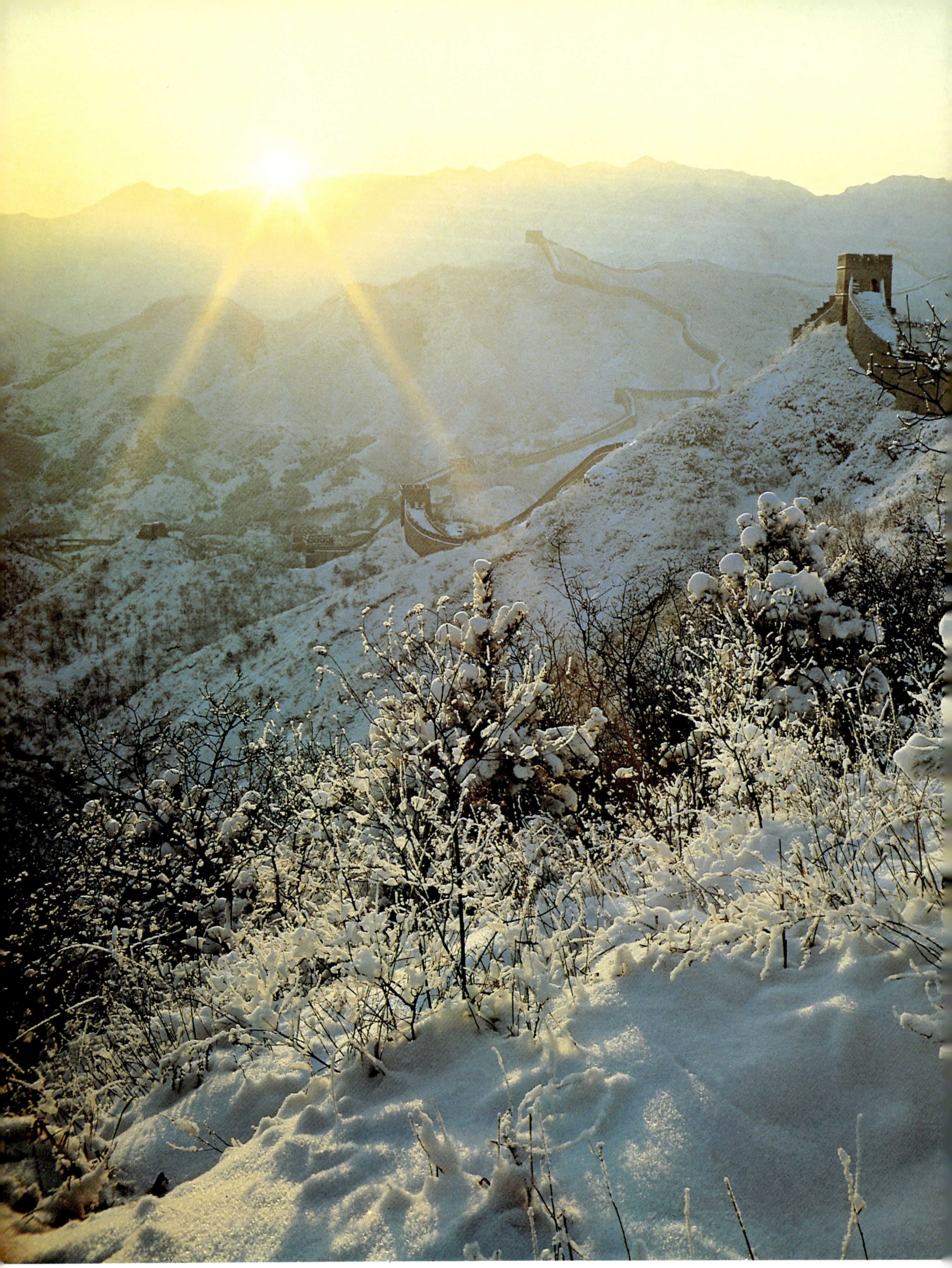

5. 八达岭雪霁
5. Badaling Great Wall

6. 不到长城非好汉
6. One who fails to stand on the Great Wall is not a true man

7. 游人如织
7. Throngs of tourists

Spectacular Scenic Sights of Beijing

8. **长城夜景** 夜幕中的八达岭长城，在彩色灯光的映衬下愈显雄奇秀美。
8. The Great Wall by night

9. 长城秋色
9. The Great Wall in autumn

10. 崇山峻岭上的长城

10. The Great Wall winding over lofty mountains

11. 金山岭、司马台长城 金山岭长城位于北京密云区和河北省滦平县交界处，司马台长城是金山岭长城的一部分。这段长城建在陡峭如鱼脊般的险峰之巅，攀登犹上"天梯"。

11. Jinshanling and Simatai Great Wall Jinshanling Great Wall runs along the border between Miyun District, Beijing, and Luanping County in Hebei Province. The Simatai section was built over precipitous and perilous peaks.

12. 烽燧夕照
12. The Great Wall at sunset

13. 八达岭晨曦

13. Badaling Great Wall at dawn

明十三陵平面示意图
Map of the Ming Tombs

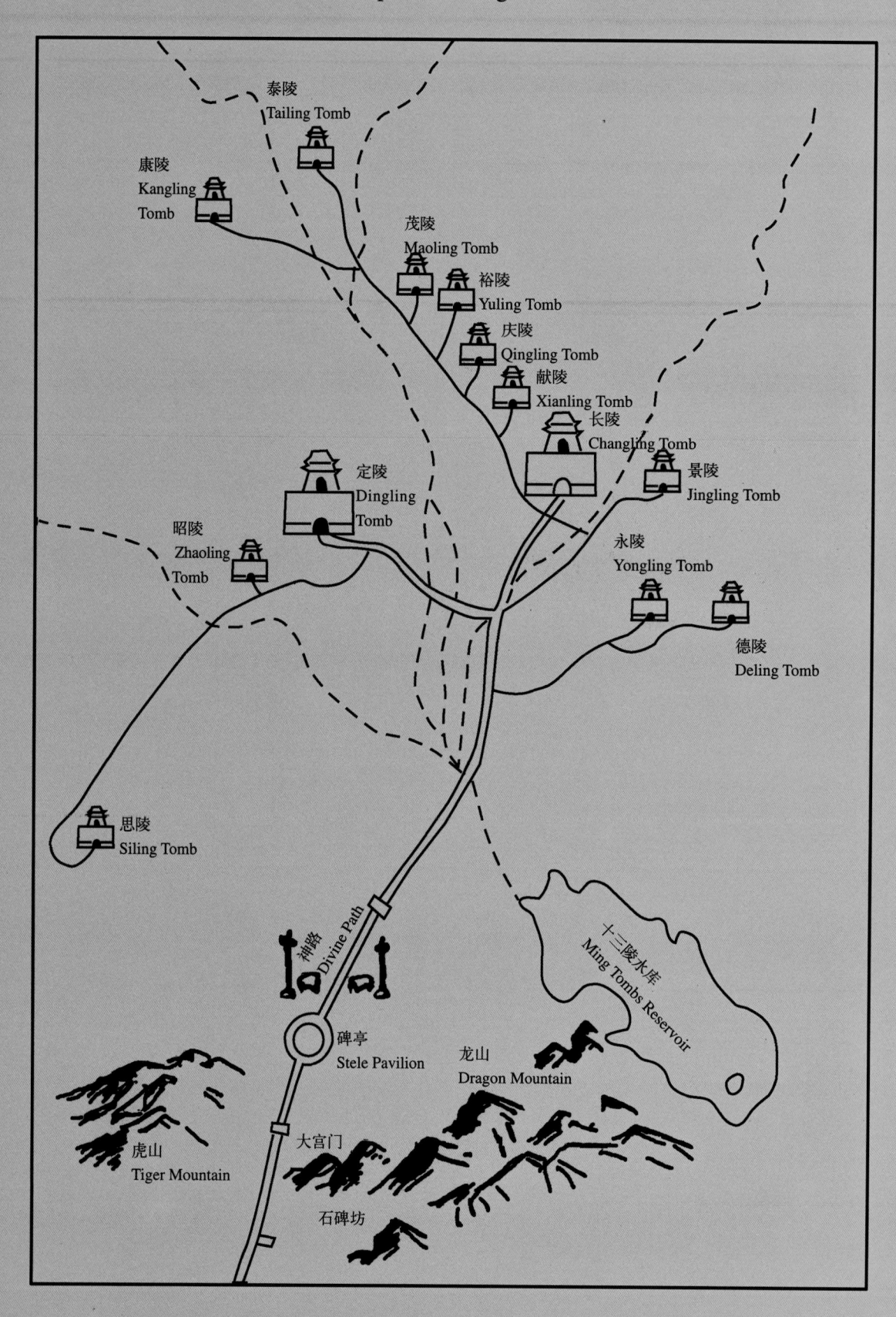

明十三陵

　　明十三陵位于北京北部昌平区的天寿山南麓，距北京市区40余公里。因陵区葬有自明成祖朱棣（1402-1424年在位）以后的明代十二个皇帝，故称明十三陵。2003年7月，明十三陵被联合国教科文组织列入《世界遗产名录》。

　　中国封建帝王大多迷信，在位时就开始为自己选地建陵。明成祖朱棣多次派员协同术士风鉴先生到北京郊区寻找"吉壤"，最终朱棣决定在黄土山建造皇陵，并且改黄土山为天寿山。此后，明朝历代皇帝（除景泰帝外）的陵寝便陆续建在了这里。

　　明十三陵陵区总占地面积达40平方公里，东、西、北三面环山，中间为盆地，南有龙虎二山镇守左右，陵墓由北向南依次而建。各陵均按明朝皇室规制营建，总体布局与皇宫的"前朝后寝"格局无异，陵前建神道、碑亭、石牌坊等，陵寝地宫上建宝城、明楼，形成了一个庞大而森严的建筑群体。

　　迄今为止，明万历皇帝朱翊钧的陵墓定陵是13座陵中唯一被考古发掘的陵墓。

THE MING TOMBS

　　The Ming Tombs are 40 kilometers north of Beijing City on the southern slopes of Tianshou Mountain. They are the burial ground of 13 Ming Dynasty emperors. In July 2003 the site was designated world cultural heritage by UNESCO.

　　China's emperors were very superstitious, and sought suitable resting places while still on throne. Ming Emperor Zhu Li frequently dispatched officials and geomancers in search of "auspicious soil" in Beijing's suburbs. Eventually he decided to build his tomb on Huangtu Mountain, and changed its name to Tianshou. Other than Emperor Zhu Qiyu, all the succeeding Ming emperors built their tombs here.

　　The whole area covers 40 square kilometers. It has mountains to its east, west and north, and Dragon Mountain and Tiger Mountain are on either side of its southern entrance. The 13 tombs go from north to south. They are arranged in the manner of the Imperial Palace, with the administration area in the front and living quarters at the rear. In front of the tombs are divine passes, stone archways and stele towers. The Precious City and Ming Tower stand over the Underground Palace.

　　Dingling, tomb of Emperor Zhu Yijun, is the only one of the 13 tombs that Chinese archaeologists have excavated.

1. **长陵** 是明十三陵中建陵最早、规模最大的一座，是明成祖朱棣及其皇后的陵寝。长陵的主要建筑从前往后依次是棱恩门、棱恩殿、明楼和宝城。

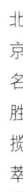

1. Changling   The first and largest of the 13 Ming tombs, this is the resting place of Emperor Zhu Li and his empress. Its main structures are the tomb gate, Ling'en Hall, Ming Tower and Precious City.

2. 长陵明楼 明楼是每一座陵墓的标志性建筑，均建于砖砌的宝城之上。

2. Ming Tower of Changling

3. 祾恩殿 又称"享殿"，是帝、后或旧朝遗官祭陵的地方。现只有长陵的祾恩殿还保存完好。

3. Ling'en Hall This is where the living emperor, his empress and officials paid respect to the late emperor buried in Changling. It is the only one of its kind intact in the area.

· 3

· 4

4. 神路石像生　又称"神道"，是通往明十三陵陵区的主要道路。路的两旁有石兽、石人雕塑，其中石兽12对，有狮、獬豸、骆驼、象、麒麟、马各两坐两立，石人6对，有勋臣、文臣、武将3种，都是全身朝服，手执笏板，拱手站立。这些石雕完成于1435年，形象生动、逼真，每座石雕均用整块巨石雕成。

4. Divine Path　This is the main path to the Ming Tombs. On both sides of it are stone sculptures of human figures and animals. Of these, 12 pairs are animals, including lions, camels, elephants, horses, xie and qilin (animals in Chinese mythology), one of each pair crouching and the other standing. The six pairs of stone figures are of three categories: officials with meritorious records, civil officials and military officials, all in court dress and holding a huban (a slim tablet held by officials when received in audience by the emperor) to their heart. These sculptures were carved in 1435, each from a whole piece of stone.

Spectacular Scenic Sights of Beijing

5. **定陵** 是明神宗朱翊钧及其两个皇后的陵墓，也是明十三陵中唯一被考古发掘的陵墓。定陵地宫中出土的随葬品达3000余件，现已建成定陵博物馆。

5. **Dingling** This is the tomb of Emperor Zhu Yijun and his two empresses. It is the only one of the 13 Ming tombs to have been excavated for archaeological purposes. Over 3,000 funereal objects were unearthed from the tomb, which is now the Dingling Museum.

6. 定陵明楼
6. Ming Tower of Dingling

7. 定陵宝城城台
7. Precious City of Dingling Tomb

8. 定陵地宫入口
8. Entrance to the Underground Palace of Dingling Tomb

9. **地宫甬道** 通往地宫各殿的隧道
9. Underground Palace tunnels   These lead to various chambers in the Underground Palace.

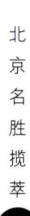

10. 地宫 殿中有三个汉白玉宝座。宝座前有供桌和长明灯。三个宝座中两个是为两个皇后设置的，一个是为皇帝置备的。

10. Underground Palace This contains three white marble thrones, one for the emperor, and two for his empresses. In front of the thrones are alter tables and Everlasting Lamps.

11. 棺椁 置于地宫后殿中。地宫后殿是地下宫殿的主要组成部分。殿中棺床的中央置放着朱翊钧的棺椁，其两个皇后的棺椁分别置于左右，其余是装满殉葬品的红漆木箱。

11. Coffins These coffins are in the rear hall of the Underground Palace. Emperor Zhu Yijun's coffin lies in the center of a platform, and those for his two empresses on his either side. Also on the platform are lacquered boxes filled with sacrificial objects.

12. **金冠** 又名"翼善冠",和乌纱翼善冠一样都属于皇帝常服之制。金冠全部用金丝编制而成,中国只此一顶。

12. **Gold Crown** Part of the emperor's death apparel, and woven in gold thread, it is the only one of its kind in China.

13. **凤冠** 为皇后礼服之制。皇后在上朝大典时所戴。整个凤冠上有5000余颗珍珠,150余块宝石。

13. **Phoenix Crown** This was worn by the empress at grand ceremonies. It is adorned with more than 5,000 pearls and 150 precious stones.

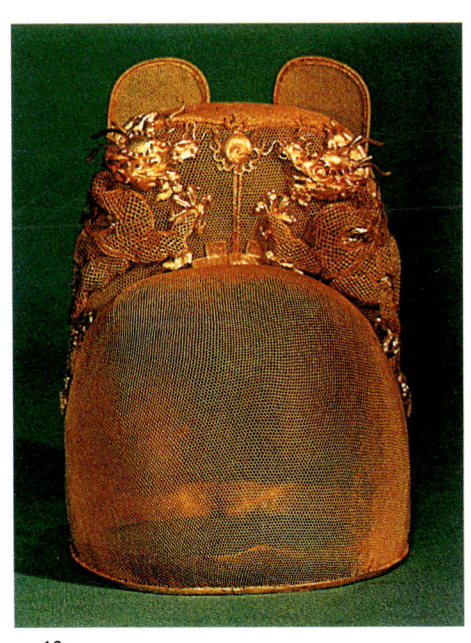

· 12

· 13

· 11

北海平面示意图
Map of Beihai Park

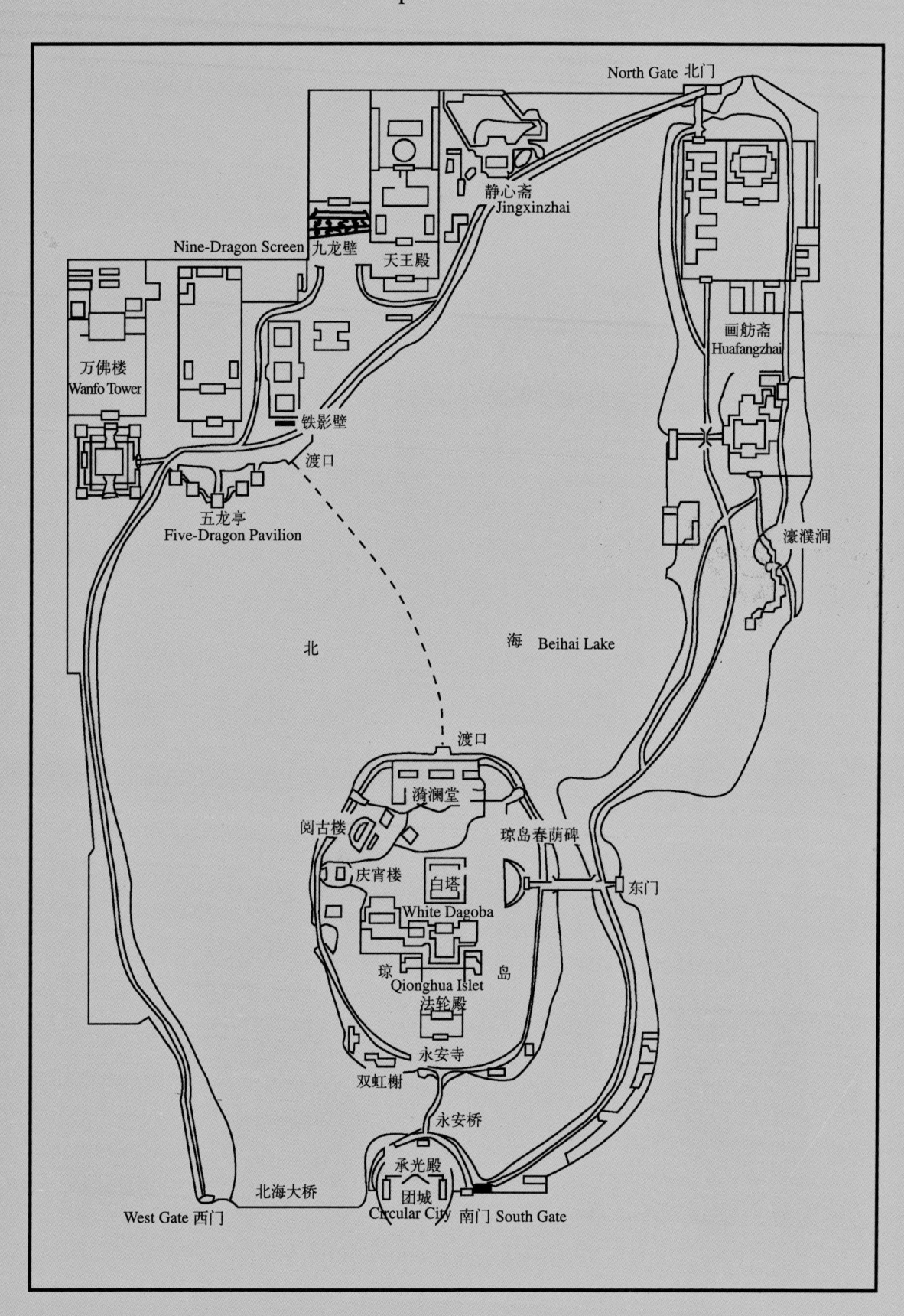

北海公园

　　北海公园位于北京内城中央,隔桥与中南海相望,东南角是故宫,东边与景山公园相邻,是内城中别具特色的皇家园林。

　　北海公园的建造历史可追溯到唐代(公元618-907年),当时在北海公园附近建造了大片园庭,统称海子园,包括了如今的北海公园。以后,经过辽、金、元、明、清各个朝代的修葺和扩建。新中国成立以后,进一步疏浚三海,修整、增加设施,就有了今天美丽宜人的北海公园。

　　北海公园总面积约66.68公顷,以琼华岛为主体,白塔为中心,四周亭台殿阁隐现于万绿丛中。主要景观有团城、琼华岛和东岸、西北岸景区,大都自成体系,其中的"琼岛春荫"是著名的燕京八景之一。

BEIHAI PARK

　　The imperial garden is at the center of the inner city of Beijing. Across a bridge it faces Zhongnanhai, the Forbidden City is to its southeast, and Jingshan Park is to its east.

　　The park was originally built in the Tang Dynasty(618-907), along with many other gardens in this area that were called collectively Haizi Garden. Reconstruction and expansion were carried out in the following dynasties. After the People's Republic of China was founded, the government dredged the lake, renovated the buildings, and installed facilities in the park.

　　Covering a total area of 66.68 hectares, the park's scenic spots include Qionghau Islet, Tuancheng (Circular City), and the Eastern and Northwestern Shore areas around the White Dagoba. "Spring Shade on Qionghua Islet" is one of the eight best sights of Beijing.

1. 远眺琼华岛 岛上山顶的藏传佛教白塔，是北海公园的标志性建筑，传说可镇京师水患。

1. Qionghua Islet   The Tibetan-style dagoba on the islet is the main landmark of Beihai Park. It was believed to protect Beijing against floods.

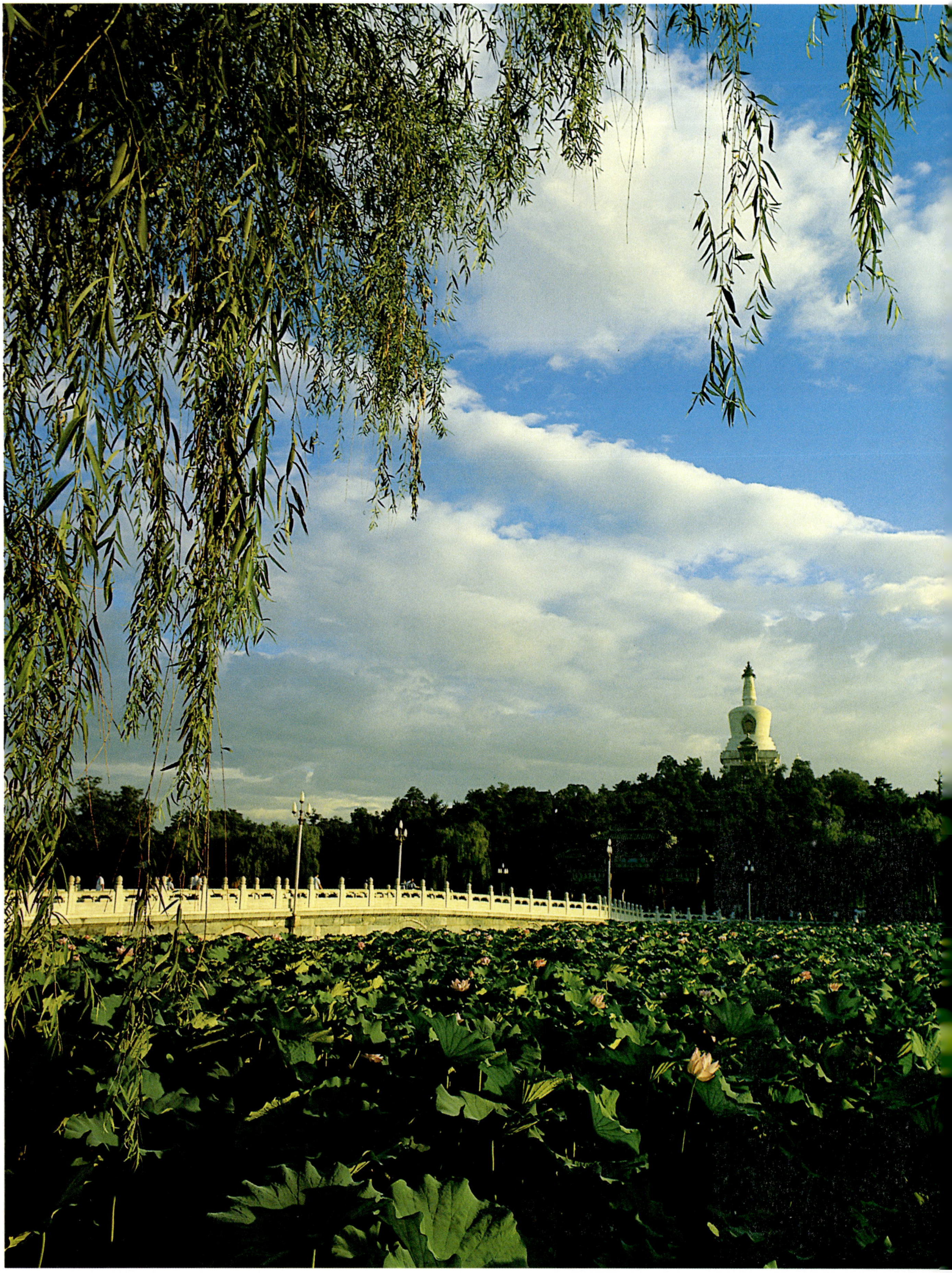

2. **太液荷香** 北海旧称"太液池",内植荷花,盛夏时节池内荷香四溢。

2. **Fragrant Lotus Blossom on Beihai Lake** In former times the lake was also called Taiye Pool. In summer, when lotuses come into bloom their fragrance exudes over the whole lake.

3. **五龙亭** 亦称"天地亭",位于北海北岸,是帝后垂钓、赏月、观焰火的地方。中间龙泽亭为皇帝垂钓处,左右各两亭是文武官员陪钓处。

3. **Five Dragon Pavilions** From these pavilions on the northern shore of the lake the emperor and empress fished, admired the moon and enjoyed fireworks. The one in the middle is for the emperor, the others for accompanying officials.

4. 白塔、善因殿 白塔建于白塔山顶，为藏式喇嘛塔，塔高35.9米。塔下善因殿为上圆下方的琉璃建筑，墙壁四周镶嵌的千手千眼佛像达445尊。殿中央供奉有文殊菩萨化身铜像，俗称"镇海佛"。

4. White Dagoba and Shanyin Hall The lamaist dagoba is on top of Baita Hill. It is 35.9 meters high. At the foot of the hill is Shanyin Hall, a structure of glazed tiles. Its upper part is round, and the lower part is square. Around its exterior are 445 statues of the Buddha of One Thousand Eyes and One Thousand Hands. There is also a copper statue of Manjusri Bodhisattva in the hall.

5. 画舫斋 是春雨林塘院内临池正殿。清代皇帝常约集名画家进园作画，作品集中陈列于此，故名"画舫斋"。

5. Huafangzhai This is the main hall in the Chunyulintang Courtyard, which overlooks a pool. During the Qing Dynasty the emperor often invited famous painters to come to the park to draw. He would exhibit their works in this hall.

6. 静心斋 位于北海北面，南临太液池，始建于明代，1759年扩建。原名"静清斋"，是太液池中的园中小园，人称"乾隆小花园"。

6. Jingxinzhai (Studio of the Rested Heart) Looking out over the lake in the south, the studio was first built in the Ming Dynasty, and was expanded in 1759. It is also known as the Little Garden of Qian Long.

7. 承光殿 位于团城城台中央,殿内供奉有整玉雕琢的白玉佛一尊。

7. Chengguang Hall This stands at the center of the Circular City, and in it is a white jade statue of Buddha.

8. 团城 位于北海公园南门西侧,被称为"北京城中之城"。此处辽、金、元时建有小岛,后又建造了城郭和仪天殿。明代重建改为承光殿,并用砖筑成近圆形城台。城高5米余,面积4500平方米。城台上建有殿宇、房屋上百间,还有参天古松柏。

8. Tuancheng (Circular City) Standing at the southern gate of the park, this was an islet during the Liao, Jin and Yuan dynasties. During reconstruction in the Ming Dynasty its round brick base was built. It is more than five meters high, and occupies an area of 4,500 square meters. On the base are over a hundred of halls and houses and ancient pines and cypresses.

9. **承光殿白玉佛** 白玉佛高1.5米,头顶及衣褶嵌有红绿宝石,清光绪年间由缅甸赠送。

9. **White Jade Buddha** This 1.5-meter-high statue is inlaid with red and green gems. It was a gift from Burma to Qing Emperor Guang Xu.

10. **琼岛春荫**　位于白塔东北面，倚晴楼南面，是北京著名的"燕京八景"之一。

10. **Qionghua Islet**　The islet is northeast of the White Dagoba and south of the Yiqing Tower. Spring Shade in the Qionghua Islet is one of the best sights of Beijing.

11. **九龙壁**　建于明代万历年间，壁高5米，长27米，厚1.2米，用彩色琉璃砖砌成，两面各有9条浮雕蟠龙，戏珠于天空、海水之间，造型生动，是中国现存的三座九龙壁之一。

11. **Nine-Dragon Screen**　Built in the Ming Dynasty with glazed color bricks, the screen is 5 meters high, 27 meters long, and 1.2 meters thick. There are nine relief dragons playing with pearls in clouds and waves on either side. It is one of the three extant nine-dragon screens in China.

• 10

北京名胜揽萃

Spectacular Scenic Sights of Beijing   113

雍和宫平面示意图
Map of Yonghegong Lamasery

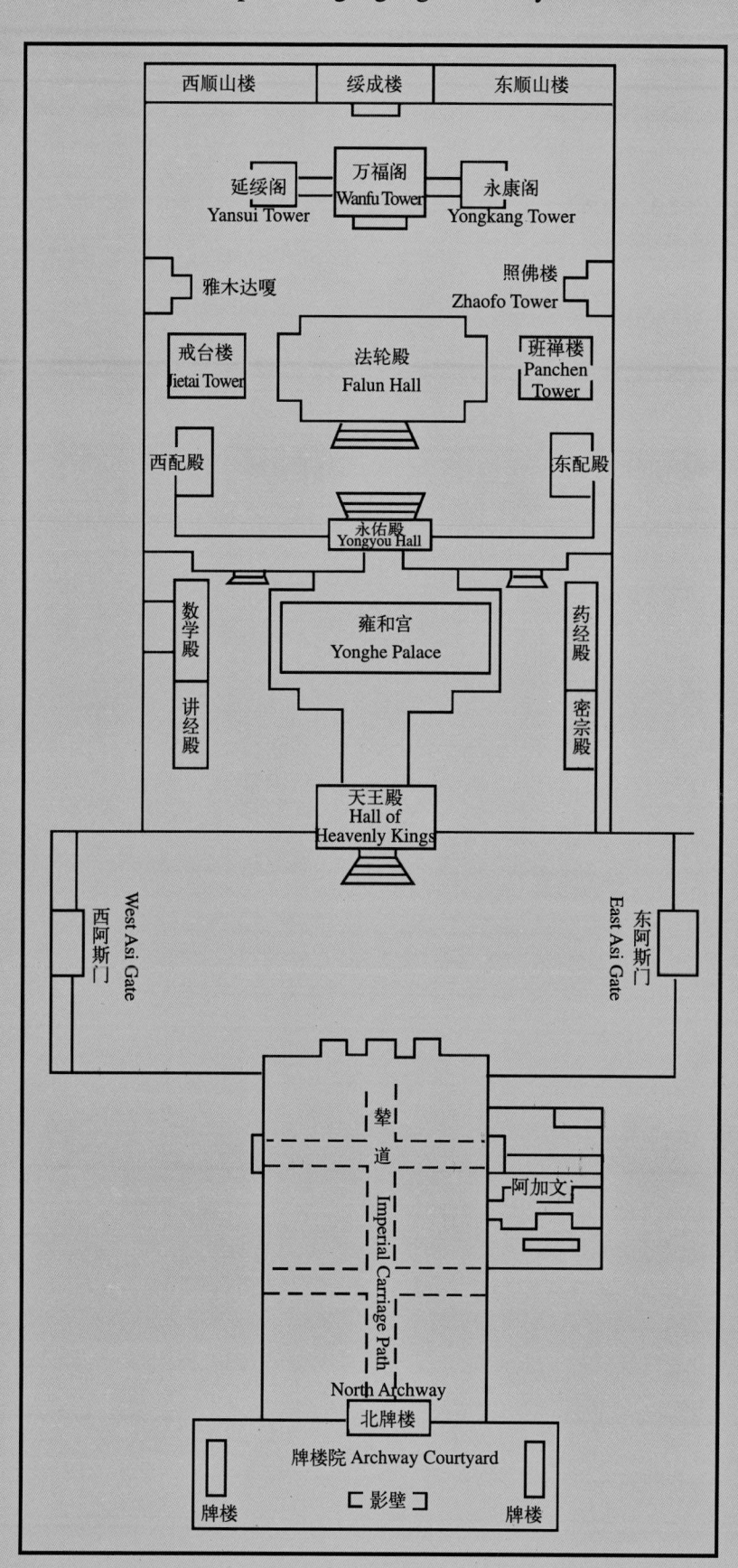

| 西顺山楼 | 绥成楼 | 东顺山楼 |

- 延绥阁 Yansui Tower
- 万福阁 Wanfu Tower
- 永康阁 Yongkang Tower
- 雅木达嘎
- 照佛楼 Zhaofo Tower
- 戒台楼 Jietai Tower
- 法轮殿 Falun Hall
- 班禅楼 Panchen Tower
- 西配殿
- 东配殿
- 永佑殿 Yongyou Hall
- 数学殿
- 雍和宫 Yonghe Palace
- 药经殿
- 讲经殿
- 密宗殿
- 天王殿 Hall of Heavenly Kings
- 西阿斯门 West Asi Gate
- 东阿斯门 East Asi Gate
- 辇道 Imperial Carriage Path
- 阿加文
- 北牌楼 North Archway
- 牌楼院 Archway Courtyard
- 影壁
- 牌楼
- 牌楼

北京名胜揽萃

Spectacular Scenic Sights of Beijing

雍和宫

　　雍和宫位于故宫的东北方向，始建于1694年，占地面积约6.6万平方米，原为康熙第四子胤禛的雍亲王府。雍正登极后改名为雍和宫，1744年改为藏传佛教格鲁派寺院。由于雍和宫曾经是帝王行宫，所以备受清廷重视，成为清政府管理藏传佛教、处理蒙藏问题的政治机构，具有内地藏传佛教的中心地位。

　　雍和宫建筑群融合了满、汉、藏、蒙风格，由七进院落五重大殿、东西配殿和四大僧院组成，尽显佛门圣境之庄严而不掩皇家宫院的帝王之气，是北京现存规模最大、保存最完好的藏传佛教寺院。

　　作为中国著名的藏传佛教艺术博物馆，雍和宫藏有10世纪至20世纪初中国各个朝代的佛像，以及14世纪早期以来的唐卡、法物、法器、纺织品、民族生活用品、明清家具等大量文物。

YONGHEGONG LAMASERY

　　Northeast of the Forbidden City, and first built in 1694, Yonghegong Lamasery occupies an area of 66,000 square meters. It was the residence of Qing Emperor Yong Zheng while he was crown prince. After he ascended the throne, Yonghegong was given its present name. It became a temple for the Gelug sect of Tibetan Buddhism in 1744. Having been an imperial palace, the Qing rulers continued to use Yonghegong. It served as the political organ responsible for Mongolian and Tibetan affairs, and was also the center for Tibetan Buddhism in inland China.

　　Yonghegong buildings display Manchu, central Chinese, Tibetan and Mongolian architectural characteristics. The complex is composed of seven courtyards, five main halls with side halls to the west and east, and four lamas' quarters. It is the largest, best-preserved temple of Tibetan Buddhism in Beijing.

　　Also a museum of Tibetan Buddhist art, Yonghegong houses Buddha statues from dynasties of the 10th to early 20th century. Its cultural relics date from the early 14th century, and include Thangkas, musical instruments used in religious rituals, textiles, articles of daily use and furniture.

1. **雍和门** 原为雍亲王府大门。改庙时把雍和门被扩展成天王殿，殿内供奉4尊巨大的"四方护法神"，俗称"四大天王"。

1. **Yosnghe Gate**   Formerly the front entrance to Prince Gong's mansion, at the time Yonghegong became a temple the area behind the gate was extended and built into the Hall of Heavenly Kings. It houses giant statues of the Four Heavenly Kings.

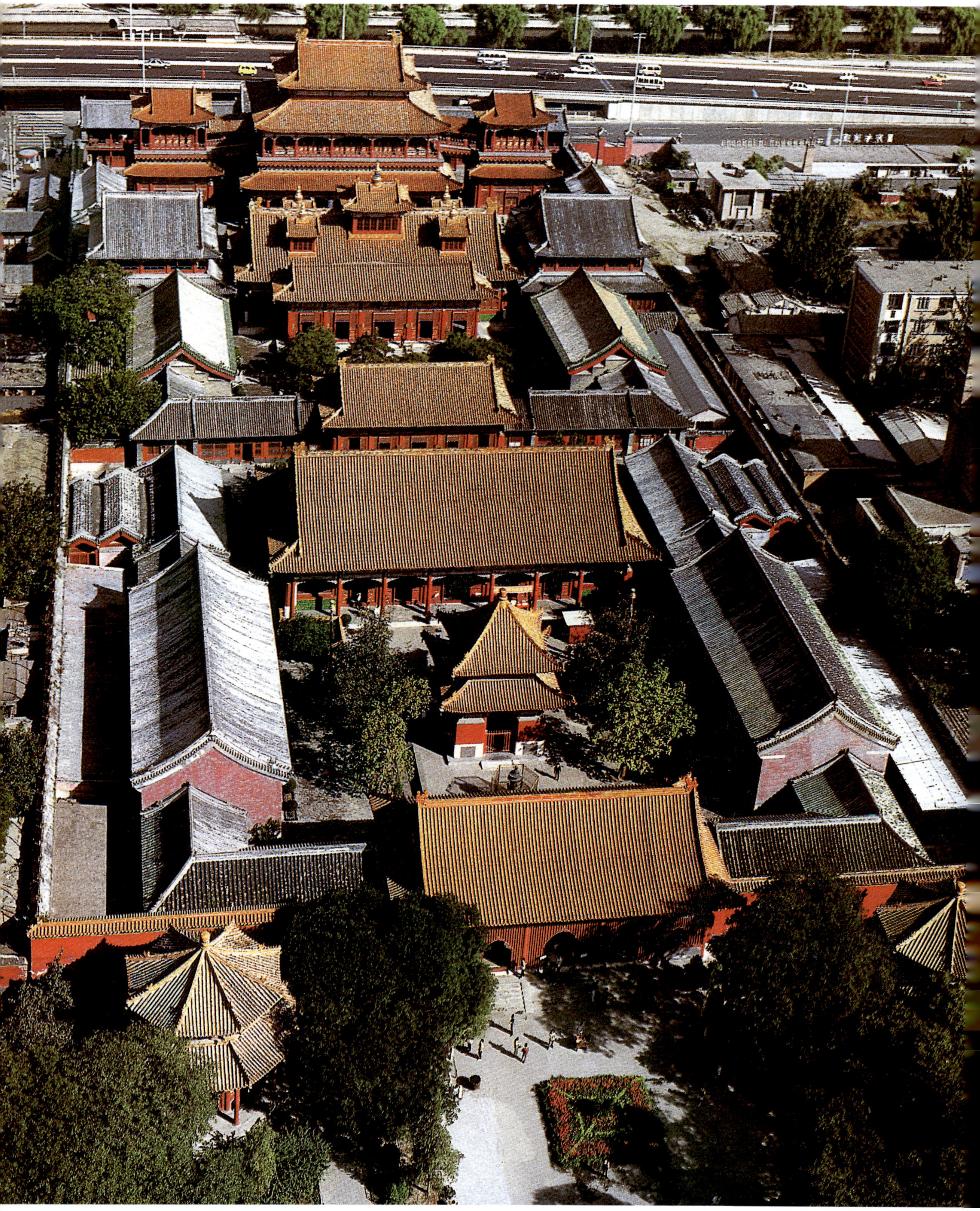

2. **雍和宫全景** 雍和宫是北京现存规模最大、保存最好的一座藏传佛教寺院。

2. A bird's-eye-view of Yonghegong Lamasery Yonghegong Lamasery is the largest, best-preserved temple of Tibetan Buddhism in Beijing.

3. **牌楼院** 雍和宫南院是一片广场,正北和东西大门处各有一座高大的五彩牌楼,故得名牌楼院。三座牌楼建于乾隆九年(1744年),各高10米有余,叶青石基座,全部用名贵的金丝楠木制成,雕刻彩绘精细,上覆黄琉璃瓦歇山顶,整座牌楼雄伟壮观。北牌楼为三间四柱九顶,东西牌楼为三间四柱七顶。

3. Archway Courtyard In the southern part of Yonghegong is a courtyard enclosed by three tall painted archways to the north, east and west. Built in 1744 during the reign of Emperor Qian Long, the archways are more than 10 meters high. They are made entirely of gold-veined nanmu (a precious fragrant timber), and have hipped gable roofs of yellow glazed tiles. The arches are delicately carved and painted and stand on stone pedestals. The northern archway incorporates three gates, four pillars and nine roofs, while the western and northern archways each have three gates, four pillars and seven roofs.

4. 雍和宫大殿　原为雍亲王胤禛会见文武大臣的地方，称"银安殿"。改建成寺庙后，殿内主供三世佛。

4. Main Hall of Yonghegong　This is where Emperor Yong Zheng met with court officials when he was crown prince. On the complex being made into a temple it became the Trikala Buddhas shrine.

5、雍和宫内景

5. Inside the Main Hall of Yonghegong

· 6

6. **金贲巴瓶** 又称"金瓶",是乾隆皇帝为"金瓶掣签"定夺西藏"转世活佛"而特制的,共两尊。一尊藏雍和宫,另一尊藏西藏大昭寺内。

6. **Gold Urn** The gold urns, made at the behest of Emperor Qian Long, are used in the lot-drawing ritual that identifies the soul boy. One urn is kept in Yonghegong, and the other in the Tsuglagkhang Monastery in Tibet.

7. 法轮殿 是雍和宫内最大的殿堂之一，也是僧人举行佛事活动的场所。殿顶上有五座天窗式的暗楼，每座暗楼仿西藏寺院建筑风格，顶上有镏金舍利宝塔，宝塔上悬挂着许多风铃，整体建筑融会了汉藏建筑艺术风格。

7. Hall of Wheel of the Law One of the largest halls in the compound, this is where lamas enact religious rituals. On its roof are five clear-story-patterned attics in the style of a Tibetan monastery. They are topped with gilt copper pagodas from whose eaves hang copper bells. The hall is a combination of Han and Tibetan architectural art.

8. 法轮殿顶
8. Roof of Falun (Wheel of the Law) Hall

9. 法轮殿内景　殿内供奉藏传佛教格鲁派创始人宗喀巴大师像，高6.1米，铜质镏金。
9. Inside the Hall of Wheel of the Law
In the center of the hall stands a 6.1-meter-high copper statue of Tsongkhapa, founder of the Gelug Sect of Tibetan Buddhism.

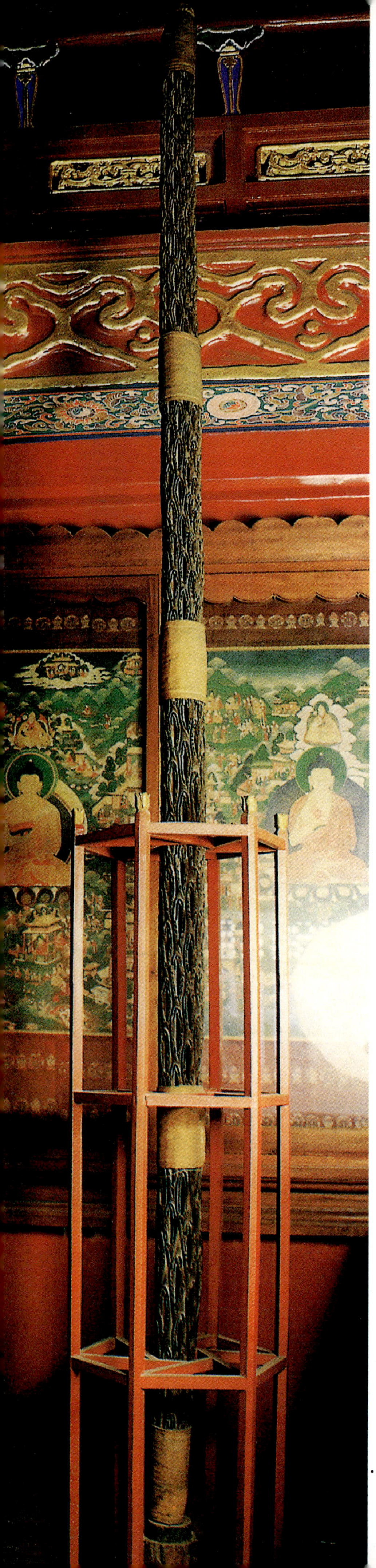

· 10

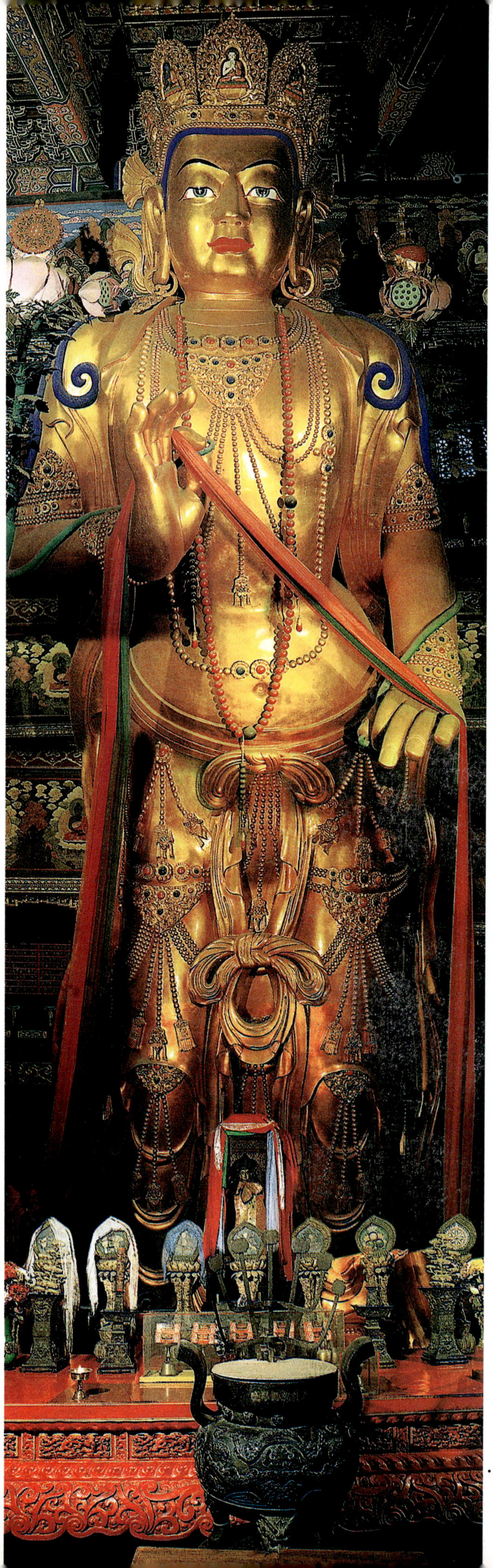

· 11

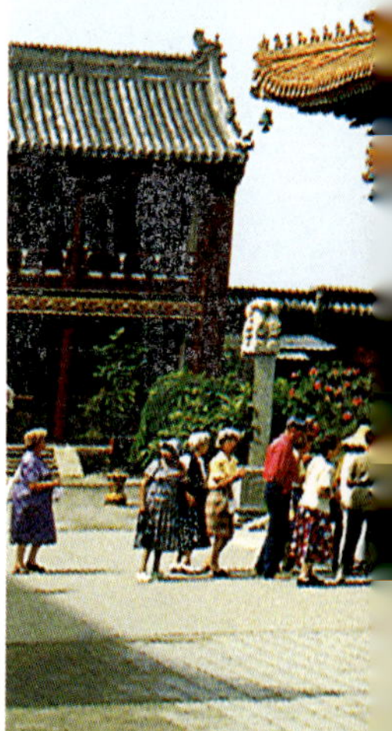

10. 凤眼香 是两株有亿万年历史的古生物化石，高3.9米，上面天然生成的花纹如同凤眼，故名"凤眼香"。

10. Fengyanxiang (Phoenix's Eye Incense) Measuring 3.9 meters in height, this pair of fossils dates back billions of years. The name Phoenix's Eye refers to veins in them reminiscent of eyes of phoenix.

11. 慈氏菩萨 藏语称"强巴"，又称万达拉佛。这尊立身佛像是由直径3米的整棵白檀香木雕成，地上18米，地下8米，被誉为雍和宫木雕三绝之一。

11. Maidala Buddha This 18-meter-high statue is carved out of a whole piece of white sandalwood, 3 meters in diameter and 26 meters long, 8 meters of which extends underground.

12. 万福阁全景 又名"大佛楼"、"万佛楼"，建于乾隆十三至十五年（1748-1750年）。高23米，飞檐三重，东西两侧各有一条悬空走廊，称"飞廊"，与永康阁和延绥阁相通。

12. Wanfu Tower This 23-meter tower with its three tiers of eaves is also known as Dafo (Giant Buddha) Tower and Wanfo (10,000 Buddhas) Tower. It was built between 1748 and 1750 during the reign of Emperor Qian Long. One corridor links it to the Yongkang Tower to its west and another to the Yansui Tower to its east.

13. 大威德怖畏金刚本尊 大威德金刚为密乘本尊之一，是文殊菩萨在密乘无上瑜珈部所显的愤怒本尊像。

13. Statue of Yamantaka Yamantaka is one of the main Gods of the Esoteric Sect of Buddhism.

14. 时轮金刚本尊　又称时轮王佛，他头有4面，代表四季，24臂代表二十四节气。

14. Time-wheel Vajra　Also called the Time-wheel Buddha, the vajra has four faces, representing four seasons, and 24 arms, indicating the 24 solar terms.

· 15

128 Spectacular Scenic Sights of Beijing

· 16   · 17

15. 旃檀佛   铜质站像，又称"昭佛"。传说释迦牟尼为母说法，弟子们请佛站在水边，由画师照水中之影绘形，故衣纹有水纹状，并依画雕成了有水纹衣的佛像。

15. Copper Tongtan Buddha Statue   It is said that as Sakyamuni stood by a river, talking to his mother about Buddhism one day, his disciples had a painter portray him from his reflection in the water. This was the image on which his statue was based, and why the folds of Sakyamuni's clothes appear to ripple.

16. 昭佛楼佛堂   乾隆皇帝之母钮祜禄氏皇太后烧香拜佛的佛堂。整个佛龛用金丝楠木雕成，雕有大小金龙99条，造型逼真，结构严谨，被誉为"神工鬼斧"，是雍和宫木雕三绝之一。

16. Tongtan Buddha Tower   This is where Emperor Qian Long's mother worshiped Buddha. The whole niche is made of gold-veined nanmu wood, and carved with 99 dragons of various sizes. It is one of the three wood carving masterpieces to be seen in Yonghegong.

17. 五百罗汉山局部   五百罗汉山被誉为雍和宫木雕三绝之一。山由紫檀木精雕细镂而成，山景清晰，层峦起伏，气势磅礴。高约5米，长3.5米，厚0.3米。山上500个罗汉像由金、银、铜、铁、锡5种金属制作，千姿百态，栩栩如生。

17. 500-Arhat Mount (section)   This is one of the three wood carving masterpieces to be seen in Yonghegong. The mountain, made of red sandalwood, is 5 meters high, 3.5 meters long and 0.3 meters thick. The 500 lifelike arhats on it, made from gold, silver, copper, iron and zinc, are of diverse physiognomies and postures.

· 18

18. 塔型法轮　永康阁内的塔型法轮为八角形二层佛塔，每层供奉 4 尊无量寿佛，雕刻精细，形态生动。转动法轮，寓有"法轮常转，佛法久住"之意。

18. Pagoda-shaped Wheel of the Law　The wheel of the law in the Yongkang (Perpetual Health) Tower is an octagonal two-tier pagoda. In each tier are four statues of the Buddha of Infinite Life that turn the wheels of the law, indicating that "the wheel of the law always runs, and the power of Buddha is eternal."

19. **唐卡《吉祥天母》** 唐卡泛指供奉在藏传佛教寺院内的各种佛画。内容以佛像、佛教故事为主，一般绘于布上，或用刺绣、织锦、帖花等技法制作。画的风格独特，色彩对比强烈，艳丽逼真。唐卡源于印度，唐代传入中国西藏，明初格鲁派的创立使其有了空前发展，形成了藏传佛教的一大特色。

19. Thangka of the Auspicious Goddess of Heaven A thangka is a painted scroll displayed in the temples of Tibetan Buddhism whose theme is generally Buddha and Buddhist stories. They are in exotic styles and bright colors that are woven, embroidered, or done in appliqué. Thangkas originated in India, and were introduced to Tibet during the Tang Dynasty. At the beginning of the Ming Dynasty the Gelug Sect was founded, and Thangkas became a distinct feature of Tibetan Buddhism.

· 20

20. **金银法轮** 佛之教法谓之法轮。
20. **Gold and Silver Wheels of the Law** Buddhist doctrines are referred to as wheels of the law.

21. **金刚铃杵** 藏传佛教僧人所用之法器。
21. **Diamond Bell and Club** Ritual instruments in Tibetan Buddhism.

· 21

22. **宝瓶** 内盛甘露，供僧人作法事时加持、浴佛等用。
22. Sacred Vase This vase contains water used for Buddhist rituals.

23. 跳金刚驱魔神舞 雍和宫每年正月二十九日至二月初一都要举行祈愿法会，其中有跳金刚驱魔神舞的宗教仪式，俗称"打鬼"。打鬼时，殿上燃灯数百盏，吹奏乐器，众多喇嘛戴面具舞蹈跳跃，场面十分隆重，充满神秘气氛。

23. Vajra Expelling Devils Dance   Yonghegong Lamasery enacts Buddhist rituals from the 29th day of the first month to the first day of the second month of the lunar year. The Vajra Expelling Devils Dance, also known as Beating Ghosts, is one. This is an impressive and mystical rite. Hundreds of lights illuminate the hall, and a large group of masked lamas dance to music played on ritual instruments.

24. 阎魔护法舞
24. Bull-head Protector Dance

25. 送祟 打鬼的最后仪式是将装有"妖魔"的三角盒送到牌楼院的柴堆上焚烧。
25. Sending away Devils The last Beating Ghost ritual is held in the Archway Courtyard, when a triangular box containing devils is burned.

图书在版编目（CIP）数据

北京名胜揽萃／尚礼，王占军，殷秦编著.
北京：新星出版社，2003.7
ISBN 7-80148-547-5

Ⅰ.北... Ⅱ.①尚...②王...③殷... Ⅲ.名胜古迹－
简介－北京市－汉、英 Ⅳ. K 928.701

中国版本图书馆 CIP 数据核字（2003）第 056131 号

编　审：于明新
编　著：尚　礼　王占军　殷　秦
责　编：殷　秦
翻　译：孙　雷
译　审：Pamela Lord
设　计：姜　江　王　勇　鲁　东
摄　影：董宗贵　高明义　狄　华　张兆基　刘启俊
　　　　罗文发　姜景余　左远波　张文忠　陈杰安
　　　　尚冠华　皮大维　王　勇　尚　礼　袁　苓

北 京 名 胜 揽 萃

尚　礼　王占军　殷　秦 编著

新星出版社出版发行

北京百万庄大街24号　　　邮　编：100037
北京华新制版新技术有限公司制版
北京新华彩印厂印刷
开　本：889×1194mm 1/16　印　张：8.5
2003 年 7 月第 1 版第 1 次印刷
ISBN 7-80148-547-5/Z · 548
定　价：68.00 元

17-CE-6702P